CW00926641

The life of Reilly

Part One

The life of Reilly

A fictional account

Prologue

England, 1760;

The Industrial Revolution comprises a long series of interwoven events and is inextricably linked to the story of coal. The period can be considered to have run from approximately 1760 to around 1840, twenty years into the reign of Queen Victoria.

The many technological advances of the period created a huge demand for coal, the fuel source which was needed to power the new industrial machines such as the steam engine. In a single century annual coal production would rise from around five million tons ten years before the revolution, to an incredible twelve fold output of sixty million tons by 1850.

From coal one could produce coke, a pioneering method of smelting developed fifty years earlier.

Coke could be used to turn iron ore into iron.

Near Telford, England 1781;

The world's first cast iron bridge is completed to cross the gorge at Ironbridge where it spanned the river Severn. Its aim was to provide a suitable crossing of this busy river to support the growth in industry around that area. The bridge gave its name to the town that evolved as a result and can properly be acknowledged as the cradle of the industrial revolution.

The various uses to which iron could be used continued to be explored by other innovators of the time. It was of course used extensively to build the machinery that filled the new industrial factories of Britain.

As demand for iron rose so too demand grew for coal.

To meet the demand for fuel the mines grew in number, went deeper underground and became more dangerous.

With more mines came more miners.

Parkinson

Houghton le Spring, Durham, England, 1791;
Oddly enough our story doesn't start with a Reilly.
A decade has passed since the iron bridge paved the way for an explosion of innovation and some two hundred miles north of Telford, somewhere in the County of Durham a baby girl is born.
As our first encounter with her is to be found in the census of 1841 nothing is known for certain about her family origins or even her surname. We do know however that the baby is named Isabella.
Although not carrying the surname Reilly she is to become an important link in our story. When she grows up she will go on to marry into the Parkinson family. Her name will also feature as a family name through future generations.
The surname Parkinson is what is known as a 'patronymic', a name that is based on the name of a person's father, in this case usually with the name of Peter or its diminutive Parkin. Originally an English name concentrated along the east and north coast of England it also found its way into Scotland and, since the 17th century, into Ireland.

Paris, France, 1792;
A year has passed since the birth of Isabella and almost ten years have passed since America, in 1783, aided by French forces gained independence from British rule and became a Republic.
But the cost to France of its support to the youthful American nation in its struggle against the British had proved incredibly costly. By 1788 the Royal treasury had been declared empty and the ensuing economic policies bred discontent widely among the French people, leading to revolution a year later.
So it is that in France of 1792 we find a twenty three year old army officer who has fought toward the birth of another Republic. He gave his support to the French Revolution and dreamt of a French Republic no longer serving a monarchy that was disconnected from the people of France.

The young officer in question had been born in August 1769 on the island of Corsica, which had recently been annexed by the Kingdom of France, into a family of minor Italian Nobility.

Recalled to Paris by his superiors the young officer arrives there to witnesses the departure of the King of France, Louis XVI, after the assault on the Tuilleries.

A year later, on January the 21st 1793 Louis, who had ironically supported the revolution in America in support of republicanism would lose his head on the guillotine as the result of a revolution in France to support the same call for change.

The young army officer, although he will not be quite as young as the king when he dies, will die on the 5th of May 1821 at the age of fifty two.

Before that however he would become known across the world as Napoleon I, Emperor of the French.

Dublin Castle, Ireland, 1792;

In the same year that the Kingdom of France continued to evolve painfully toward being a Republic, a process that would separate the heads from the shoulders of royalty and nobility alike, we find another twenty three year old army officer – this one an Ensign in the British Army – who was serving in Ireland as an Aide-de-camp to the Lord Lieutenant of Ireland.

The ensign had been born in Dublin in May of 1769, a mere three months before Napoleon, into an aristocratic Protestant family. This young army officer, in contrast to our French army officer, will die on the 14th of September 1852 at the age of eighty three.

Before that he would be known as Field Marshal Arthur Wellesley (1st Duke of Wellington, KB, GCB, GCH, PC, FRS).

Reilly

County Cavan, Ireland, 1793;

Two years after the birth of Isabella the focus of our story shifts across the sea to Ireland where we will meet the first Reilly to appear in our story.

Reilly as a surname is an Anglicised version of O'Reilly (meaning descendent of Raghailleach). It is of Irish origin and most concentrated around the counties Cavan and Westmeath. Although now a widespread name it is still to be found mostly in the vicinity of its ancestral home.

And so, back to our story.

Seven years before the new century would arrive, in the same year that the King of France loses his head and departs this life, a boy is born into a farming family in County Cavan. The boy's name is John Reilly.

But being a newborn he was blissfully ignorant of the turmoil brewing across Europe or indeed of the decades of turmoil that would rage across the face of the world during his allotted time on Earth.

If his parents could talk directly to us across the generations however they would probably speak of their great hopes of a fine new future for their young son, somehow expecting that a new century would miraculously herald a new beginning.

The miracle of a new born life seldom leads to logical thought. As parents are wont to believe, they would see in the birth of their son a brighter future for him and for their family line. One that had been denied to them. How this was to come about they neither knew nor cared, they simply believed that it would. From the moment that John smiled his first smile, took his first step and spoke his first word their lives were completely dedicated to their first born son and to their growing family. They were as happy as their circumstances allowed. The perpetual political and military machinations of the wider world impinged only dimly on their small corner of it.

London, England, 1793;
Back across the Irish Sea, King George the third had held the crown of both Great Britain and Ireland since 1760.

For over two hundred and fifty years Ireland had shared a King with England – ever since Henry the VIII (in 1542 in fact when an act of parliament established a personal union between the countries), the very monarch who had separated England from the Catholic church and opened the door to allow Protestantism to flourish in the country. However there was continued discrimination against the Irish Catholic population by the protestant English and Scottish settlers. Having a king in common had not brought the peoples of his domains any closer. Rather, these settlers had systematically confiscated land across the country of Ireland in a succession of so-called 'plantations'. In a truly Machiavellian scheme England had replaced the previous Irish Catholic ruling classes with an imposed English Protestant one. This had of course resulted in a deeply engrained bitterness against English rule – one which resulted in persistent dreams of a self determining land of their own – on the part of Irish catholic tenants. Those dreams were of a time they could only hope would one day come. A day when the yoke of British burden would be finally shaken off.

Looking across at events in America and France made more than one Irishman believe that dreams could indeed come true.

County Cavan, Ireland, 1796;
John Reilly, now three years old, remained far too young to be aware of the rumours of rebellion spreading across the country. It was said during furtive conversations that the Republican French were sailing with military support – amounting to almost fifteen thousand soldiers – to help the Irish in their struggle against the continued English dominance of their land.

But he was still a boy and he was old enough to smile and wave at the soldiers, resplendent in their uniforms, as they marched past on their way south (note 1). The young boy remained unaware of the sullen reception that the smart column of soldiers were getting from the older members of the local population, including his own parents, as they passed through the lanes that wound past the farm. John merely saw the spectacle, the bright colours, and the rhythmic music that kept the soldiers marching in step with each other.

The soldiers that John watched marching on their way to defend the shores against a French invasion were not however an English regiment. They were members of the local Cavan Militia. Raised from local Irish volunteers, much to the disgust of the local population.

The regiment was marching to form part of the force being assembled by the British to meet the expected French forces. They were being sent south to help repulse the anticipated landings at Bantry Bay on the windswept coast of Cork.

In the end invasion failed.

Yet it was not defeated by military intervention but instead by nature. Defeat had come with the advent of severe winter storms; the worst recorded for almost one hundred years. After a week of being unable to land their forces, the remaining ships of the French fleet – those that had not already foundered and wrecked on the unforgiving rocks lining the coastline of the bay - scattered and made their way back to France.

Ireland, 1798;

Two years later, John now being five years old, had not only been too young to appreciate the events at Bantry Bay but was now also unable to comprehend the next momentous upheaval to take place during his young life.

In May 1798 the Irish rose up in Rebellion.

Despite the previous failure to provide support to the planned rebellion of 1796 the French had remained encouraged enough to make a further attempt. This time their efforts met with more success. They managed to land two thousand troops in support of the uprising.

For four glorious months it seemed that it might succeed.

But once again defeat was the outcome.

As a consequence, as the decade drew wearily to a close, what had started as a bitter disappointment at the outcome of the rebellion had grown and festered until it became a fresh wound in the collective consciousness of the people of Ireland – as did the resentment of the role of the local Cavan Militia in supporting the English to suppress the hopes that the rebellion had carried (note 2).

The fact that the local Regiment had fought against its own countrymen - at the battles of Arklow and at Vinegar Hill, before helping the British under Lord Cornwallis to finally put down the rebellion against the combined French and Irish forces at Ballinamuck – only served to deepen the distrust between the local population and the militiamen.

County Cavan, Ireland, 1800;

A scant year later a new century began but local sentiment toward the Cavan regiment declined even further as they continued in service to the crown even as the acts of Union of 1800 changed the relationship between Great Britain and the Kingdom of Ireland. The acts created the United Kingdom of Great Britain and Ireland. They came into force on 1 January 1801.

Despite this turn of events John Reilly's parents could only continue to hope that despite the new born United Kingdom the future would still see their dreams of a better life for their son come to fruition.

But what could they and the people of Ireland really expect?

The British appeared practically invincible.

Despite having lost their American colonies they continued to rule supreme across every ocean and in all other corners of the world. Apart, that is, from mainland Europe where France was spreading her influence at an alarming rate. So concerning was this that in 1803 Britain took up arms yet again against her old enemy, with whom they had in fact been in an almost constant state of war since 1792.

Off the south west coast of Spain, 1805;
After two years of constant war and a naval blockade of Europe the war against the forces of Napoleon and his Spanish allies reached a pivotal event. The Royal Navy further secured its unassailable dominance of the seas when Vice-Admiral Horatio Nelson (1st Viscount Nelson, 1st Duke of Bronté, KB), led twenty seven British ships against a joint French and Spanish fleet of thirty three ships of the line, (which included the Spanish ship, the Santisima Trinidad, the largest ship in the combined enemy fleet, towering above the others with four decks and carrying 136 guns. HMS Victory, Nelson's flagship by comparison was a 100 gun first rate, while the Bucentaure, the flagship of his French opponent Vice Admiral Villeneuve mounted 86 guns) and achieved a resounding victory at the Battle of Trafalgar.

While the little Admiral lost his life in the closing stages of the battle Nelson's success resounded across Europe and ensured that the French would be unable to assemble a powerful enough fleet to invade England by crossing the channel. Only two years earlier in a response to the House of Lords, the First Lord of the Admiralty, Lord St. Vincent, had prophetically announced; 'I do not say that the French cannot come, I only say they cannot come by sea.'

But the war with France took its toll upon English resources and the unquenchable thirst for men to maintain its Navy did not help matters, eventually initiating another war with America in 1812.

The United Kingdom of the Netherlands (Belgium), 1815;
On the 18th of June 1815 Napoleon and Wellington, the erstwhile junior army officers whom we met in 1792, were now both fully forged in the furnace of war and met at last on the battlefield.

Napoleon had won many of his battles, but Wellington had never lost.

The battle took place in the fields and countryside south of a town called Waterloo. To put the battle into some perspective however, the combined fleets facing each other at Trafalgar mounted more guns than were employed at Waterloo and Gettysburg added together.

Wellington's victory in this encounter effectively ended the French domination of Europe.

County Cavan, Ireland, 1818;

For the majority of common folk the events of the wider world would continue to have little direct impact. They still had to work, pay rent and feed their family. Often in that order of priority.

As day turns to night, and night inevitably turns to day, so too did John Reilly's life cycle inexorably through childhood into adulthood. His parents, though farm workers themselves, did not have the means to support him once he was of working age, regardless of their hopes for a brighter future – one that the new century had so far failed to deliver. So John sought work as a farm labourer and dreamed of having his own farm one day (note 3).

While in his early twenties he met an older woman who captured his heart from their first encounter. He was sure that his parents would not wholeheartedly approve of his liaison with a woman eight years his elder, but the difference in age meant nothing to him. Her name was Elizabeth Farrelly and over the following years John and Elizabeth's relationship flourished.

But John was reluctant to take the next step and propose marriage until he was in a better position to support both Elizabeth and any plans they had for a life together and, one day, a family.

Eventually, through constant hard work, John managed to secure a very small tenancy on an estate owned by an absent English landlord. Nevertheless this small but vital step was sufficient to allow him to propose to Elizabeth at last.

Elizabeth, overjoyed, immediately acquiesced and they married in 1818 when John was twenty five years old and Elizabeth was thirty three.

London, England, 1820;

George the third had suffered from an unknown illness for the latter part of his life which often exhibited itself as something similar to bi polar disorder. A serious relapse in 1810 resulted in the Prince of Wales, his son, becoming Regent. Once established the regency was to last for the next ten years. In 1820 when the tormented King eventually died, after a rule of some sixty years, his son took over the throne from his father to become George IV.

County Cavan, Ireland, 1830;
After twelve years of marriage John and Elizabeth Reilly live in the townland of Corr, in the Parish of Killashandra which forms part of the Barony of Tullyhunco. They have had three children in this time; Catherine, born 1825, James, born 1827 and John, newly born 1830.

London, England, 1830;
William the IV takes over the throne from his older brother and is to reign for the next seven years until 1837.

County Cavan, Ireland, 1833;
John Reilly may have been his parents first born as well as carrying their hopes for a better future, but he had always felt less successful than his younger brother Phill, despite his best efforts at improving his situation (note 4).

In this year, 1833, fifteen years after John had wed Elizabeth, Phill Reilly married his childhood sweetheart Bridget. They were both twenty two years old at the time.

After the service ended, John and Elizabeth Reilly stood outside the church with the crowd of extended family and well wishers to welcome the newly married couple. The bells rang loud and clear and even on a cold autumn day the warmth of the young couples happiness could not be dampened.

Phill had managed to acquire a sizeable holding which greatly overshadowed that of his older sibling John, who, now eighteen years his elder was still struggling to make ends meet.

After a prolonged round of farewells Phill handed his bride up onto the seat of the trap before jumping up to sit alongside her. The smiles on the faces of the happy couple were echoed by everyone in the crowd as he took the reins and crop in hand and set the pony in motion. They both waved happily to John and Elizabeth as they left the church behind them and headed off along the winding lane to reach the small farmhouse that was to become their home.

England, 1837;
When her uncle William IV dies, a young girl eighteen years of age becomes next in line for the throne and begins her reign as Queen of the United Kingdom of Great Britain and Ireland.
She would go on to exceed the previous longest reign and rule for the next sixty three years.
So began the Victorian era.

Ashington, Northumberland, England, 1840;
Ashington grew from being farmland in the early 1800's to become a large coal mining village by 1840.
By the late 1840s Ashington the landowner, The Duke of Portland, had built housing for his mines to encourage workers escaping from the famine in Ireland to settle there and work in his mines. He had also given a few local men the right to mine coal on a Rental and Royalty Payment Agreement.
These men founded what was to become the Ashington Coal Company, changing the original rural hamlet into a one-industry town of over twenty-five thousand people in just over forty years.
At the peak of coal mining in the area Ashington was thought to be the largest coal mining village in the world.

County Cavan, Ireland, 1841;
After eight years of married life John Reilly's brother Phill and his wife, both now twenty nine are well established and happy at their farm. The newly born decade saw them with a growing family of their own. They had settled in the nearby townland of Coradownan in the same parish as John. Phill and Bridget's family now consisted of; Patt, born 1835, Catherine, born 1837, Anne, born 1839, and Bridget, born 1840.
In addition they had agreed to have John and Elizabeth's son, their nephew James (note 5), who was now 14 years old, stay with them

to learn his trade. John's own small tenancy was hardly sufficient to feed the whole family and afforded little diversity in terms of farming education for James.

Phill came to appreciate his nephew as if he were his own son while he stayed with them and was pleased that his older brother had agreed that he move in to the household to help with the increasing level of work on the farm. James had also done well at school and could read with ease. He was thankful for his uncle's support and enjoyed his time on the farm. But while he was grateful for this period of his life within uncle Phill's family he of course missed his own family, even though they lived less than ten miles away.

While attending a get together with friends and family James does not realise it at the time but he meets his future wife Ann Wilson, who is a young girl six years his junior. The Wilson's are family friends and Ann often visits her relatives who live near to where James now lives. Over the coming years they would meet on numerous occasions at church or at events such as the annual fair or on high days and holy days outings. Of course as Ann is presently only a girl of eight years at this time James simply finds her very annoying.

Parkinson

Houghton le Spring, Durham, England, 1841;
The baby girl we saw born in 1791 is now known by her married name of Isabella Parkinson and is 50 years old.

She is a widow struggling to maintain her family. The Parkinson household live at Rainton West, Houghton le Spring, Durham, England.

Isabella was secretly grateful that her eldest son, twenty year old William Parkinson, had yet to find a wife. The money that he contributed to the household coffers helped support both herself and William's brothers and sisters; John Parkinson, fifteen years old, Elizabeth Parkinson, nine years old, Edward Parkinson six years old, and Isabella Parkinson, who was five.

But while Isabella struggles to lead a household on her own a prospect of both happiness and security enters her circumstances. As the year draws to a close Isabella meets and marries Edward Rawling. After the constant struggle of recent years she harbours hopes that the stability of having a husband heading the household will provide a more stable future for her family as well as happiness for herself.

Reilly

Ireland, 1845;

A strange agricultural disease, phytophthora infestans, accidentally reaches Ireland from the Americas. It also affects mainland Europe but the special circumstances in Ireland mean that the disease will cause devastation. James Reilly is eighteen years old when the potato blight reaches the shores of Ireland where it arrives on the heels of the stories of its terrible effects in America and its spread across Europe. Across the country each year would be followed by another year of failed potato crops. The withered leaves and the rotted tubers would become a common sight and everyone would learn to live amid a stench that was stomach churning and terrible.

A typical tenant farmer, such as James' own father, had barely half an acre to support his family. Across the nation, until now, the only viable crop to do so reliably had been the potato and as a result a significant proportion of the population since the early 1800's had relied almost solely on this food source as their staple diet. Even then, most families lived on the edge of starvation during ordinary times so this crisis was devastating in its effect. Eventually it led to over one million deaths. A further million people would chose to leave the country rather than starve.

The bitter irony was that other crops and foodstuff continued to be available throughout this terrible period. But these were cash crops for export and profit for the landlords – the Irish people literally starved in the midst of plenty.

Things were made worse by the unbending English economic policy of laissez faire and a refusal to provide financial or other aid until it was too late and inadequate.

County Cavan, Ireland, 1850;

The country was now five years into what would become an almost decade long famine.

James Reilly was now twenty three years old and Ann, now seventeen, has thankfully begun to draw his attention away from the terrible situation he and all of the people he knew were living through.

Their relationship has burgeoned over the last ten years from one initially based on childhood tolerance on the part of James, through to mutual companionship and finally into a serious relationship (note 6).

James thought that this relationship was wholly one of deeply shared friendship.

But what James was not aware of was that from an early age Ann had determined that James would become her husband.

And once Ann made a decision she stuck to it.

Parkinson

Houghton le Spring, Durham, England, 1851;
The Parkinson household had moved to Market Place, Houghton le Spring, Durham following Isabella's marriage but her security was relatively short lived. Less than ten years after marrying Edward Rawling, Isabella found herself a widow once again, but she was now sixty years old.

Although her older children had left home she still retained the company of Elizabeth, who had also taken the name Rawling and was now twenty one years old. Young Isabella Parkinson (and Edward also still live with their mother and now Edward works as a coal miner.

The family household was completed by another Isabella Parkinson, a three year old granddaughter (Elizabeth's daughter) and a further newly born granddaughter, Margaret Ann Parkinson. It is unclear from the records whether Margaret Ann is the offspring of Elizabeth or of her unmarried younger sister Isabella.

Also, although the census records Elizabeth Rawling as being married there is no record of her husband or the co-incidence of taking the surname Rawling. In 1851 she is recorded as being born in 183 therefore Elizabeth would have been eighteen years old when Isabella was born.

However, in the previous census of 1841 Elizabeth is recorded as being born in 1832 and if this were the case she would have been sixteen when her daughter was born (note 7).

As will be seen later, this could potentially be the first in a series of family skeletons unearthed – or simply be a transcription error.

Reilly

County Cavan, Ireland, 1853;
James Reilly is now twenty six and Ann, once more staying with her relatives, is no longer a girl and is most definitely a woman twenty year of age. They are at the annual county fair but have an argument (note 8).

If anyone asked James later what the argument was about he would not have been able to reply. He still held confused feelings about the woman that his best friend had recently become while she continued to remind him of the young girl that he has grown up with.

Perhaps the argument was simply because the long years of struggle against poverty and famine had finally worn James down. The effects of the famine continue to be felt across the country and locally many people known to James have either died or already left to seek better prospects elsewhere. He even knew some who, unable to feed themselves or pay the rent, had simply walked away from their homes rather than wait for starvation or eviction to overtake them.

The argument with Ann had perhaps simply been an expression of how he felt, a sudden outpouring of pent up frustration that he could not combat the situation in which he found himself.

In response to her own frustration Ann simply ended the argument with a stamp of her foot and stormed off without a backward glance, hoping and expecting that James would understand the signals she was trying to give him and follow her.

But he does not.

Worse, he does not even realise that we was supposed to.

Unable to resist any longer Ann stole a glance over her shoulder and looked back to where she had left James standing, in time to see him enter a tent where strong ale was on sale. He was seeking temporary consolation in the oblivion that the drink would provide.

From a distance Ann continued to keep a watchful eye, in dismay, as he took far too many beers and drank himself into a deeper state of confusion and morose self pity.

For a fleeting moment Ann felt a mild sense of triumph that she had managed to stir such strong emotion in James and thrilled at the fact that she would be able to use the same power over him in the future to ensure that she secured him as a husband. She knew in her heart that he was a good man and that these fits of frustration with their life in these bleak times was usually fleeting. She was sure that he would suffer no more than a hangover and be back to his normal self very soon.

Then her eyes opened in horror as she watched a recruiting party for the hated Cavan Militia – lately reformed as the 101st Regiment – approach the tent.

Fairs such as these were fertile recruiting grounds even for the unfashionable regiment; especially if suitable men could be prevailed upon while under the influence of strong drink, which would miraculously be topped up as the unwitting candidate listened to the wild claims of untold riches and of a grand life fit only for the very best of men.

The recruiting sergeant was an old hand and experienced in all the tricks of his trade. He carefully placed his men at the exits to the tent and then entered the interior with only his drummer boy at his side and a stream of shining coins that jingled enticingly in his hand. Even at a distance Ann could see the cheerful banter begin as the sergeant passed through the tables eyeing prospective targets for his practised speeches and well rehearsed stories.

Ann started to experience a sense of panic.

She knew that in James' drunken state he could become easy prey and that it would be a simple thing for the sergeant to convince the young man that taking the Queen's shilling would be a better alternative to the constant struggle to find sufficient work on the farms – something it was becoming increasingly difficult to do in these dreadful times.

Ann hesitated a moment longer then ran through the crowds of the fair, stopping only briefly here and there to ask if anyone knew where James' father and uncle were, hoping she would not be too late.

In moments she had located the two men and breathlessly explained her fears to them.

She had to run to keep up with them as they headed for the ale tent at a brisk pace and she just arrived in time to see them drag James out, clearly unable to support himself. From within the tent she heard the sergeant's protests about the beer money that he had wasted as James was taken away before he could be talked into taking the shilling.

They sobered James up by repeatedly dunking his head in a water barrel and then holding it there until his thrashing about indicated that the cold water was forcing rapidly acquired soberness into his head. Then they dumped him unceremoniously onto the ground next to the butt.

He ruefully shook droplets of water from his hair and looked up at his father and uncle. 'Thanks,' he said, before adding with a grin, 'Although I'd have made a fine figure in the Queen's coat don't you think.'

He hadn't noticed Ann who had been peering anxiously around his father's shoulder. Which was just as well as the look on her face showed that she did not appreciate his little joke.

'It's not us you should be thanking lad,' said his father with a broad grin on his face. He nodded at the young woman behind them. 'It's her you should be saying thank you to.'

James moved his gaze to where Ann Wilson stood, as his father added, 'And if you have any sense in that thick skull of yours you should take note how clever she is – smarter than you seem to be at least...'

At that Ann Wilson decided that the time had come for her to put her foot down with a firm hand.

She moved to stand in front of the two men and, hands on hips, stared down at James before she addressed him in no uncertain terms. 'Now look here James Reilly, I've had quite enough of these goings on. It's high time that you realised that we are to be married and the sooner you understand that then the better it will be for all concerned!'

And with that she turned on her heel for a second time that day and marched off into the crowd that was gathered to watch the show.

Still in a daze James finally realised what it was that had been puzzling him. He now understood that the young woman storming away from him was no longer the friend of his youth – she was a full grown woman – and a fine attractive one at that.

'Well,' said his father, 'are you going to go after her or are you as daft as you seem to be?'

James looked up in amazement until he saw that both his father and his uncle were grinning good naturedly. Then he thrust himself onto his feet and without a backward glance ran off in pursuit of the woman he finally realised was to be his wife.

A month later he and Ann were sitting upon a dry stone wall watching the sun sink toward the far Atlantic when James turned toward her and said, in all seriousness, 'But what shall we do Ann?'

Ann gripped his hand more firmly, looked up into his eyes, but remained silent.

James continued, 'There's nothing here for us, and I want more for you than I can give here, a home, a future...'

Ann studied him for a moment longer before responding. 'We'll get married. We'll go to England, make a new life there.'

He thought about what she said and slowly he came to the same conclusion. Even though they held no love for the English he held the idea of leaving for America in lower esteem. But lower still in the present circumstances was the idea of a future in Ireland with little work or a means to support himself and Ann, let alone any family they may dream of.

Ann was right, he realised, but he hadn't really considered the first step until she had said it again. He jumped down from the wall and, kneeling took Ann's hands in his. 'Will you marry me?' he asked.

'Of course I will you silly man,' replied Ann happily, before adding, 'haven't we been engaged these last dozen tears?'

They married later that year.

Not longer after they wed, they find out that the English have joined with the French in declaring war on Russia. So begins the Crimea War.

The 101st Regiment (Cavan Militia) raises volunteers to send there and fight alongside the English, for Queen Victoria.
The war would continue until early 1856.

Embleton, Durham, England, 1859;
Shortly after they wed at Bailieborough, and having said their goodbyes to their families and friends, James and Ann Reilly gathered their scant possessions and took passage from Dublin to England, following reluctantly the exodus that had been a constant drain on the population of Ireland for the last decade (note 9).
The first leg of their journey took them to Dublin, a place bustling with people, sights and smells that a quiet country life had not equipped them to cope with. But they enjoyed their brief stay in the busy city where they passed a few adventurous days exploring before the planned voyage to England. When the day arrived they walked together down to the docks and joined a mass of people heading toward the ship tied up alongside. They held tightly to each other and their bags then climbed the gangway to the entry port on the ships open deck. They found a space on one of the wooden benches that lined the upper works of the ship and settled down to wait for the departure.
Soon they heard orders being called and watched as seaman moved purposefully about the ship, casting off and preparing to get underway. Slowly the steam packet to Liverpool prised its bulk away from the land and set off into the watery expanse that separated Ireland from the mainland of Great Britain. Grabbing James by the hand Ann pulled him to his feet and they found a space at the rails where they stood together in silence and gazed back at the coastline of their home country as it receded into the distant west and wondered if they would ever see it again.
When they landed the process was reversed until they found themselves once again in a bustling sea port with more people than they had dreamed could live in one place. They sought lodgings for the night and as they lay in bed they spoke in hushed tones about what their new life would be like.

After a tiring cross country trek they settled in Embleton near Sedgefield in the county of Durham. It proved easier to find work in England than it ever could in Ireland and the wages were better – even as a labourer rather than a farmer in his own right like his father.

The birth of their first child Mary, born in 1855 made James question further what was to be done to improve their lot. He continued to work as a labourer, and while the living was better than it had been in Ireland, it was still far from what he had hoped for.

But now, having been in England for six years the fact of being surrounded by coal mining meant that an idea was born within him that eventually would prove too powerful to resist.

During their time at Embleton he and Ann had formed a close friendship with a fellow Irish couple, Thomas and Mary Smith. This had helped them to settle in their new community but at the same time made them wistful for their previous home in Ireland.

Overall though their time at Embleton was full and content, resulting in two further bairns becoming additions to the Reilly household. Joining their older sister Mary were, Philip, born 1857 and Margaret, born 1859.

In fact both they and the Smith's had babies born in the years '57 and '59, which served to bind the families even closer in friendship.

Morpeth, Northumberland, England, 1861;

Two years after his third child was born, James Reilly, now thirty four, took what he hoped would be another improved offer of employment further up the great north road. He moved his family fifty five miles north to a farm in the parish of Hebron outside of Morpeth – Tritlington North Farm, Tritlington Holms, Tritlington (note 10).

Convincing the Smith family to come along with them, he offered that they could lodge together in the tied cottage that came with the work, until they found their own place to live (although it seems incredible to modern ideas that it would be possible to house two families in one tied cottage).

In this same year that James and Ann relocate to Northumberland they have a fourth child that April, a son whom they also call James.

Parkinson

Houghton le Spring, Durham, England, 1861;
Meanwhile, in Durham, the Parkinson household is now at Seaham Road, Houghton le Spring and has Isabella's son Edward Parkinson as its head (although we have no record we assume that his mother Isabella has died).
He is now twenty six years old and continues working as a coal miner.
But due to various circumstances he found himself caring for two children who, according to the previous census, should have been his niece and nephew yet he chose to record as; Isabella Parkinson (sister), thirteen years, born 1848, Durham and James William Parkinson (brother), two years, born 1859, Durham.
We know that Isabella was the daughter of Edward's sister Elizabeth but the mother of James William is not known.
Due to the prevailing social strictures it must have seemed to Edward that it was wiser to class his niece and her younger brother as being his siblings rather than to argue with the parish as to whether he was in a suitable position to provide for their care in the absence of their parents.

Ashington, Northumberland, England, 1867;
1867 is regarded as the date at which present day Ashington was founded. The shaft at Bothal was sunk in 1867 and soon there were five collieries in the Ashington area.
Ashington as anticipated has now grown into one of the largest towns in Northumberland – fifteen miles north of Newcastle and three miles from the North Sea – even though it hardly existed other than a small hamlet before the 1840s when the Duke of Portland began building housing to encourage workers to work his collieries.
Finding workers had been relatively simple; in addition to the many farm workers escaping the starvation in Ireland there were economic migrants from Cornish tin mines and a consequence of the industrial revolution meant that the introduction of farm

machinery had led to rural workers being made redundant and they too sought work elsewhere.

Houghton le Spring, Durham, England, 1871;
A decade later Edward Parkinson, now thirty six years old, still lives at the same location but times have moved on and he now acknowledges that his household consisted of; Philip Todd (nephew), twenty years, born 1851 and Isabella Parkinson (niece), twenty three years, born 1848.

This reconfirms that Isabella is the daughter of Elizabeth but there is no other information regarding Philip Todd. If he is a nephew he can only be the son of a married sister of Edward who presumably has met a man with the surname Todd.

But this census provides a further potential stigma to deal with in the form of another member of the household; William James Parkinson (Isabella's son), one year old.

There is no mention of the previously recorded James William (he would have been twelve years old), but the repetition of the name, although reversed, is intriguing.

Jones

Clifton, Bristol, England, 1871;

The surname Jones is an English and Welsh patronymic originating from Jon(e) and meaning John's son.

While it is especially common to find the name in Welsh families it is also commonly found in southern central England. It is in fact possibly of English origin regardless of it being predominantly found in those of Welsh extraction.

One reason for this dates from the 16th century when the Welsh had to adopt a surname system in a similar manner to that in use in England. Due to the prevalence of the name John at the time, in honour of various saints of that name, those previously known as John's son became Jones.

In England a common variation on this principle produced Johnson.

One person with this surname now plays a part in our story.

John Jones was born in 1848 in Gloucestershire, the same year as his future wife Frances Jane Heath who came from the nearby county of Somerset. He and Frances were married in the first quarter of 1870 when they were both aged twenty two.

A year after their marriage they are recorded as lodging with John's older brother at Belle Vue Place, Clifton, Bristol.

Parkinson

Houghton le Spring, Durham, England, 1881;
Another ten years pass and Edward Parkinson is now forty six years old and still lives at the same location.
There is no mention of what became of Isabella and her son but now our story is concerned with the paternal Parkinson line.
Edward has now married a woman called Ann, ten years his younger. Ann is recorded in this and subsequent census entries as being originally from London.
Unfortunately they are not to have children.

Ashington, Northumberland, England, 1887;
By 1887 Ashington had six hundred and sixty five houses in eleven long rows to accommodate the miners. The rows of colliery houses are now home to people who came from as far as Ireland and Cornwall.
As Ashington expanded the increasing number of colliery houses were built to a grid pattern with streets in the Hirst end running north to south and names after British trees. East to west streets were numbered avenues. The Hirst End was east of the railway while on the side of the line, the West End was thought of as being Ashington proper.
Due to the lack of public houses – the Duke and the mine owners were Quakers and had to date maintained Ashington as a tee total environment – a number of working men's clubs were now being built – at its height there were twenty one of them in the town.

Reilly

Seaton Delaval, Northumberland, England, 1891;

Like so many others before him James Reilly had finally swapped work on the land to work within its bowels – pursuing the greater rewards available to anyone willing to work hard, long hours underground.

He had relocated his family once again, over fifteen years earlier, to set up a new household in Quarry Row, Seaton Delaval. Seaton Delaval pit had been producing coal since 1838.

In 1891 however, James being aged sixty four finds his working life is over. Now retired from coal mining, he and Ann still count two of their children as part of their household; his daughter Catherine, who had been born in 1869 in Morpeth and his son Hugh, who followed in his footsteps and now works as a coal miner (driver), having been born at Earsdon near Seaton Delaval.

They also had their grandson residing with them at the time of the census return. He was the son of their oldest, Philip Reilly who also recorded him on the census return.

Philip Reilly, the eldest son of James and Ann, is now thirty four years of age and no longer part of his fathers household. In fact he has been married to Catherine Duffy for almost ten years now – they married in late 1879 at Chester Le Street, Durham – and they have set up their own household at Camp Terrace, Seaton Delaval not far from Philip's parents.

Having grown up at Morpeth there came a point when he too had been drawn from working on the land to follow the greater rewards afforded by coal mining leading him into the industry alongside his father (note 11).

Catherine's father had known Philip's parents when they were first in the country from Ireland and had kept in touch ever since. As Catherine had grown up she and Philip had grown closer together. She was from Houghton le Spring and had happily followed her husband north of Tynemouth after the wedding. They now had four children; eight year old Philip, born in 1883, seven year old

Catherine, born 1884, and two further boys, James, five years old and John, three years old.

Catherine's father, fifty seven year old James Duffy was also a coal miner and he too resided in the household at the time.

Parkinson

Houghton le Spring, Durham, England, 1891;
Edward Parkinson and his wife Ann lived at the same location, North Pit, East Rainton, Houghton le Spring, for a further ten years until she died in the third quarter of this year of 1891 at the age of forty six years old.
Edward is now fifty six years old and is still recorded as being a coal miner.

Houghton le Spring, Durham, England, 1892;
One year after the death of his first wife Edward Parkinson married Barbara Ellen Smith, on the 16th of July of this year.
The wedding record notes Edward marrying Ellen Smith and was recorded at Sunderland. Barbara was born Barbara Ellen Mellon in 1867, Consett, Durham. At the age of twenty six she is already a widow.
She was thirty years younger than Edward Parkinson when they married.

Houghton le Spring, Durham, England, 1893;
Almost exactly one year after the wedding, on the 6th of July of this year, James Parkinson was born to Edward and Barbara at North Pit, Hetton, Durham.
Later James would work in the pits from the age of thirteen, including; Sherburn Hill Colliery, Durham, Mainsforth, Durham and Scremerston near Berwick.

Reilly

Seaton Delaval, Northumberland, England 1893;
In the same year as James Parkinson is born, but a few months earlier, on the 5th of April a fifth child, Edward, is born to Philip and Catherine Reilly.

Hardy

Ashington, Northumberland, England, 1893;

A girl is born one day after James Parkinson entered our story.

Frances Hardy is born to Ralph and Isabella Hardy on the 7th of July. Both parents are from Bothal near Ashington.

Later in life she will go on to marry James and become Frances Parkinson.

Ralph is a coal miner and also a band master. Nearly forty years later, retired and a widow, he will be found living at Chester le Street in the household of one of his other children, Frances' younger sister Deborah.

Hardy is one of a number of surnames derived from nicknames originally based on characteristics. Originating from old French and Middle English it was a nickname for someone who was brave or foolhardy.

Smith

Morpeth, Northumberland, England, 1895;

Two years after Edward Reilly was born, Elizabeth Nicholson Smith is born to Richard Major Smith and his wife Isabella.

She is christened on the 21st July 1895 at Bothal.

Later in life she will go on marry Edward to become Elizabeth Nicholson Reilly.

Smith as a surname originally derived from any form of metal worker and also from those who used the output from a smith, for example soldiers, where the word smith further derived from 'to smite'. The greatest concentration began in the region of Aberdeenshire.

Smith is the fifth most common surname in Ireland. In Irish it is Mac an Ghabhain (MacGowan) meaning son of the smith — its translation to Smith became widespread, particularly in County Cavan where the sept originated and were one of the most powerful families. A sept is an English word for a division of a family, especially of a Scottish or Irish clan.

The vast majority of the family in Cavan anglicised their name to Smith.

Parkinson

Houghton Colliery, England, 1901;
In the previous century, almost forty five years earlier in 1857, Houghton Colliery had received a Royal Visit.
The then Prince of Wales descended the shaft and was conveyed in a coal tub, pulled by a pit pony, to the coal face where he tried his hand at coal hewing. It was quite an occasion for the town and lived long in the collective memory of its people.
This Prince of Wales was to become King Edward VII this year, taking over from his mother Victoria (he was her eldest son) in January 1901.

Houghton le Spring, Durham, England, 1901;
In the same year that Edward ascended the throne another Edward, Edward Parkinson, and his wife Barbara Parkinson now live at Pontop House, East Rainton, Houghton le Spring, Durham. Edward, although now sixty four years old is still recorded as being a coal miner.
James Parkinson, their son, is now eight years old.
Also recorded on the census return is a visitor, Alice A. Smith. Alice is 18 years old and Smith was Barbara's previous married name. One can only surmise whether Alice is Barbara's sister-in-law or her own child from her previous marriage If so she would have been sixteen when the child was born).

Reilly

Seaton Delaval, Northumberland, England, 1901;

In 1901, Philip and Catherine's Reilly household was at 8 Rouble Row, New Hartley, Seaton Delaval and now consists of seven children, all born in Earsdon which means that Philip probably worked at Earsdon Colliery for the previous twenty years or so.

The children were, Philip Reilly, born 1882, nineteen years old, a Coal miner putter below ground, Catherine Reilly, born 1884, seventeen years old, James Reilly, born 1886, fifteen years old, Coal miner sheave lad below ground, John Reilly, born 1888, thirteen years old, Coal miner driver below ground, Mary Reilly, born 1896, five years old and Joseph Reilly, born 1898, three years old.

Their fifth child, Edward Reilly is now seven years old.

Jones

Bristol, England, 1901;
After the census of 1871 we lose track of the Jones family until they reappear in the 1901 record. This tells us that John and Frances Jones had produced a son in 1875 and named him Charles Henry.
1901 finds Charles Henry married to Rosina Heale. They married seven years earlier in 1894 and now have a growing household at 3 Burton Court, Bristol. Charles is now twenty six years old and works as a labourer in the docks.
His wife is one year older than he, having been born in 1874. They have five children at this time. Their fourth child, a son also called Charles Henry Jones, is four years old having been born in 1897.

London, England, 1910;
Nine years later, when the younger Charles Henry is thirteen years old, George the V takes over the throne on the 6th of May and is styled; King of the United Kingdom and the British Dominions, and Emperor of India.
He will rule until his death in 1936.

Parkinson

Morpeth, Northumberland, England, 1911;
After the death of Edward Parkinson, Barbara Ellen Parkinson re-marries in the 4th quarter of 1906.
Five years later, in 1911, she has now also travelled the Great North Road and is living at 10 Edward Street, Morpeth.
Her third husband is called John Allen, who, at sixty five compared to her forty three years is more than twenty years her senior and works as a stone miner. He had been born at Jarrow, Durham.
Now known as Ellen, she gave John a son, Joseph Allan who was born four years previously in 1907, soon after their marriage (nine months after if we are not seeking further impropriety; however being married in the fourth quarter means at the earliest the first of October 1906. Joseph is recorded as being four years old in 1911. As the census was taken on the second of April in 1911 that means Joseph was born at the latest on the first of April 1907 – at the most this is seven months after the wedding), in East Howle, Ferry Hill, Durham, before the family relocated to Northumberland.
Ellen's other son, James Parkinson, is now 18 years old (although recorded as being seventeen as the census is taken so early in the year) and has been working for five years in the pits around Ferry Hill; at Sherburn Hill and Mainsforth, before moving up to Morpeth where he secured a job at Ashington in 1910 as a coal miner, hand putter above ground.
He has already met his future wife, Frances Hardy who was born and raised in Pegswood, near Morpeth, and who, in 1911 is working as a servant to a household in Ashington (note 12).
Perhaps in dissatisfaction at the household arrangements he also worked for a time at Scremerston near the Scottish border.

James Parkinson found life in Morpeth a little tame but he enjoyed the liveliness of the Wednesday market and the opportunity to walk along the banks of the river.
One particular Wednesday the colliery bank from Pegswood was performing in the gardens bandstand on the banks of the Wansbeck

and James stopped to listen to the stirring music played on the brass instruments.

In front of the band stood a man smartly at attention, his body hardly moving as his arm moved the small wooden conductors baton in time with the music and directing the various instruments as they ebbed and flowed through the piece.

As he looked around the crowd his gave was drawn to a young woman he judged to be about his own age.

She must have sensed his eyes on her and she looked over to where he stood – and smiled.

James thought about going over to engage her in conversation but at that moment the music reached a crescendo and stopped to the applause of the spectators.

The crowd began to disperse and when James looked again for the young woman she was standing with the band master and was deep in conversation.

James decided that he too should go and turned away to follow the crowd back through the market stalls into the centre of the market town where he would find a pub for a pint.

He didn't notice that the girl watched him depart.

Later that year he started work at Ashington colliery and struck up a friendship with one of the sons of a deputy.

Over the course of the next few months they chatted about various things and came to the subject that the household now had a young woman as a servant as his friend's mother was ill and with a household of so many sons she needed the help.

One day James walked home with his friend and had a most pleasant surprise – the servant was the young woman he had seen in Morpeth those months earlier. He wasn't going to miss out again and asked her out. She immediately said yes.

The next year he joined the army – he could no long stand living in the home of a step father. He didn't want to leave Frances but he saw no choice.

'I'll be back for you when I have saved up enough for us to get married'

It is in 1911 that James set off to enlist in the Army, choosing the Gordon Highlanders, regular recruiter from the North of England, as his regiment. He enlists as a regular at Newcastle on 24 August 1911 and is recorded as being eighteen years old.

One family anecdote insisted that he lied about his age to join up. If he was born in July 1893 (as recorded in the 1901 census and the 1939 record) he would have been of age in August 1911. However his date of birth on the 1911 census has his year of birth being 1894 which would have made him seventeen on enlistment.

Coincidentally the same applies in the case of Edward Reilly who is recorded as 1894 in the 1901 census and 1893 in the 1939 record!

James is soon sent north to Aberdeen to complete his basic training as Pte. James Parkinson 745, 1st Battalion, The Gordon Highlanders. Initially he enlists for a seven year term of service with a further five in the Reserve.

After completing his basic training at Castlehill Barracks he is transferred to Colchester where the 1st Battalion were performing garrison duty.

Reilly

Seghill, Seaton Delaval, Northumberland, 1911;
Philip and Catherine Reilly's household now resided at New Square, Seghill. Their oldest son, also called Philip and their daughter Catherine, have now left the household but the rest of the family, still living with them in Seaton Delaval are; John Reilly, twenty three years old, a coal miner hewer, Edward Reilly, seventeen years old, a coal miner siding rope boy, Mary Reilly, born 1896 and Joseph Reilly born 1889, a coal miner driver.

They also had a boarder at the time, Anthony Mullarkey, twenty two years old, a coal miner hewer from Mayo, Ireland. This would seem to indicate that connections were maintained with Ireland long after the initial wave of emigration.

Edward Reilly's older brother Philip has moved to Ashington and has married. He and his wife Ellen live at 49 Sycamore St., Hirst, Ashington and have a newborn daughter, Catherine.

Jones

Clifton, Bristol, England,1911;

Rosina Jones who was born in 1874 is now a widow aged thirty seven years old.

She is still living in 3 Burton Court, Clifton, Bristol where she is now the head of the Jones household. She has four children in her household at this time.

Charles Henry, now fourteen years old is working as an errand boy. The younger children are all still at school.

First World War, 1914;

In the Balkans on the 28th of June 1914 Archduke Franz Ferdinand, who was the heir to the Austro-Hungarian throne was shot and killed.   This event led to a series of disputes between various alliances until war was declared a month later on the 28th July 1914. Private 745 Parkinson J., Gordon Highlanders has now spent three years in the Army.

In September 1913 the 1st Battalion had been relocated to quarters in Plymouth. When war was declared they were moved to Southampton and then to France on 13 August 1914 before being sent on to the Belgian frontier just south of Mons.

By November, the Battalion was holding positions near Ypres and during a fierce German attack James was one of the wounded men when he sustained a gunshot wound in his chest. He was treated initially at a Casualty Clearing Station before being moved to a military hospital at Boulogne and then on to the UK for further hospital treatment on 23 November 1914.

Reilly

First World War, 1915;

Edward Reilly's older brother, John Reilly, joined the army during the First World War. Private 4630 Reilly J. Northumberland Fusiliers landed in France in May 1915. He originally served with the 8th Battalion but later served with the 3rd.

John died aged twenty seven on the 26th November 1915.

His name is recorded in the record set; Commonwealth War Graves Commission Debt of Honour. His grave reference is; F. 10. Ashington (St. Aidan's) Roman Catholic Cemetery, Husband of Susan Brown (formerly Reilly) of 55 Katherine Street, Ashington.

Parkinson

England, 1916;

The war had presumably intervened between the fledgling relationship formed between James Parkinson and Frances Hardy, but they had perhaps kept up correspondence – the uncertainty of life during years of war eventually meant that they married when James was on leave.

Following James' return to the UK after being shot he was being regularly medically examined before being declared fit. By April 1915 he was serving at the regimental depot in Aberdeen and was sent back to Belgium to rejoin the 1st Battalion.

On 18 March 1916 the battalion was in reserve trenches, filling sandbags, when they were shelled and suffered a single casualty. James sustained an injury caused by a shell fragment. As before, he was repatriated to the UK for treatment and then to the regimental depot in Aberdeen where he was placed on light duties to aid his recovery.

Regimental records show that he married Frances Hardy at Ashington, Northumberland on 15 July 1916.

Reilly

England, 1917;

The following year Edward Reilly marries Elizabeth Nicholson Smith in August 1917.

Their first child, a daughter, is born on the twentieth of June 1917 – two months before her parents are wed.

There is no record found of Edward having been in the forces during the war but it could explain the wedding being after the birth if he was serving and either couldn't obtain leave or the baby came early. Other suppositions are left to the imagination of the reader.

Ironically their daughter will go on to marry another Smith and by so doing revert to her mother's maiden name, on the first of September 1945 at All Saints, Bakewell – Clifford Hudson Smith who was five years her junior.

England, 1918;

The first World War – 'The war to end all wars' – ends on the eleventh of November this year.

Ashington, Northumberland, England, 1920;

Edward and Elizabeth Reilly have their second and final child, James Reilly who is born on the twenty seventh of June of this year.

France/Belgium, 1917;
James Parkinson was eventually declared fit to resume active service and he was returned to France where he was assigned to the 8/10th Battalion as one of a draft of one hundred reinforcements on 14 February 1917.
The 8/10th then saw intense front line action during many battles – the Battle of Arras, the Railway Triangle, Cavalry Farm, the Battle of Passchendaele, Frenzenberg and Langemarck.

Belgium, 1918;
Having sustained heavy casualties they were moved to reserve positions in Belgium around Ypres before moving back into France in January 1918.
By 7 June 1918, the 8/10th Battalion was significantly under strength resulting in amalgamation with the 5th Battalion.
A large number of men from the 8/10th were reassigned to other Gordon Highlanders battalions. James was transferred to the 6/7th Battalion. Again, many battles entailed leading up to the Armistice. When the Armistice was signed on 11 November, the 6/7th Battalion was at Thun-Leveque. In early December, they were moved to positions east of Mons where they remained until early 1919.

France, 1919;
In February of this year James Parkinson was now fully time served and due for discharge.
For his service during the final months of the war, James was mentioned in dispatches (MiD). In their regular reports, commanding officers submitted a listing of those men who had been nominated as worthy of a mention. Recipients of an MiD received a certificate and their name was posted in the London Gazette. No records remain to provide the reason for a MiD. These lists were published several months in arrears, particularly at the

end of the war, and in James's case probably refers to his actions at sometime during October 1918.

James was transferred to Army Reserve on 23 February 1919 to serve the balance of his original 12 year term. During his time as a reservist, James was paid 3 shillings and 6 pence a week and was required to attend 12 training days each year.

On his discharge from the Army we understand (from information in a newspaper clipping) that he went to back to life with Frances and would work in Ashington, at Ellington Colliery.

However, we know that their oldest child, James Edward Parkinson was born in Durham in 1917 and that subsequently they had two daughters while they lived at Chilton in County Durham. This would seem to support a move back to Durham almost immediately after the wedding and setting up of a household there before leaving Frances to her own devices, pregnant, before he returned to the war.

England, 1920;

In May 1920 all serving British soldiers were given a new number and James was now 2865246.

Durham, England, 1921;

Still a reservist, James Parkinson was called up again to serve in the Army because of the 1921 Strike.

After release from the Army (in August 1923) for a second time he would relocate his family from Durham back to Northumberland and go on to work at Linton Colliery, Ashington for the rest of his working life. During his working years he suffered spinal injury but still held various posts after that. He was a timber drawer at one point and later he was also a chairman of Linton branch of the National Union of Mineworkers.

James and Frances have their third child, Isabella Parkinson this year. She is born in August at Chilton near Ferry Hill in Durham. This is approximately 5 miles north west of Sedgefield.

She will go on marry James Reilly and to become Isabella Reilly.

England, 1923;

James Parkinson received his final discharge from the army on 23 August 1923. For his service, James was awarded the 1914 Star, the British War Medal and the Victory Medal. His award of MiD (mentioned in dispatches – signed by Winston Churchill, Secretary of State for war) entitled him to wear a bronze oak leaf emblem on the ribbon of his Victory Medal.

Reilly

England, 1926;
A combination of miners wage reductions and economic pressures on the coal industry led to the nine day General Strike. The day after the strike was declared there were over 1.7 million strikers supporting the 1.2 million miners involved in the dispute with the mine owners.

Wombwell, South Yorkshire, England, 1930's;
Mass unemployment that had begun in the post war decade extended into the 30's.
Many miners would travel to find employment.
In the middle of the decade Edward Reilly would relocate his family, which included a teenage James Reilly at that time, temporarily to Wombwell in South Yorkshire before returning to work in Ashington.

Jones

Bristol, England, 1931;
Charles Henry Jones is now thirty four years old and marries Elsie May Pugsley.

Bristol, England, 1933;
Two years after their wedding, Charles Henry and Elsie May Jones have twin boys. William and Raymond Jones.
After being brought up in a very poor part of Bristol and being quite a poorly child, Raymond will leave school at fourteen and go to work in a factory before he joins the RAF (At eighteen he would take the decision to sign on for three years rather than to do National Service).
He would then be stationed at Yatesbury and train as a telex operator.

London, England, 1936;
Edward the VIII is on the throne from June until he abdicated in December when George VI took over.

Green

Grimsby, Lincolnshire, England, 1937;
Janet Elizabeth Green is born to parents Jack Wilyman Green and his wife Beatrice (nee Hopper). The Greens were a Lincolnshire family and lived around Spilsby and Louth at the time, while the Hoppers, also a Lincolnshire family, lived around Caistor.
She will go on to marry Raymond Jones after meeting at a holiday camp in Paignton called The Nest just before she qualifies as a State Registered Nurse.
The surname Green was first found recorded in Kent with the earliest being around 1180. It became the family name for those who lived in or on the green at the centre of a village.

Second World War, 1939;
Two years after Janet is born, precipitated by Germany's invasion of Poland, war is declared on the 1st of September.

Reilly

Ashington, Northumberland, England, 1939;
Edward Reilly is now 46 years old and has followed his brothers to set up his own household in Ashington, at 93 Maple Street with Elizabeth.
He worked as a Colliery Stoneman (Below) at Woodhorn Colliery, Ashington.
A stoneman was a worker who dealt with stone or rock rather than coal and usually meant someone who worked on the development of a stone drivage. A drivage was a new gate road leading to the face.
He had married Elizabeth Nicholson Smith in August 1917 and their two children are now adults; Catherine A. Reilly, born 20 June 1917 and James Reilly, born 28 June 1920, a colliery putter below.
In addition they have a boarder, Elizabeth's younger brother, James Smith who is a colliery shift worker below.

Newcastle, Northumberland, England, 1939;
Edward's father, Philip Reilly, now eighty two years old is recorded as both a coal miner (retired), and widowed.
He is now living at St. Joseph's House, Westmorland Road, Newcastle.

Parkinson

Ashington, Northumberland, England, 1939;
James Parkinson is now also forty six years old and is a colliery conveyor drawer and has also settled down in Ashington. He is now living at 39 Laburnum Terrace. His wife Frances is also forty six years old and the rest of the household consists of their two daughters; Alice, born 6 Feb 1920, and Isabella, born 28 August1921.
Isabella's older brother James is twenty two and has left the household and will go on to enlist in the Army – after the war he recounts his walking the length of Italy and on as far as Ghent in Belgium.
Laburnum Terrace is a mere four streets from Maple Street.

Jones

Bristol, England, 1939;
Charles Henry Jones has been married to Elsie May Pugsley for eight years.
He works as a general labourer. The twin sons complete the household; William and Raymond, born six years before.
Ray will go on to marry Janet Elizabeth Green.

Reilly

Ashington, Northumberland, England, 1942;

James Reilly was born on the 28th of June 1920. Now aged twenty two years he marries Isabella Parkinson on the 3rd of December 1942 at St. Aidan's Catholic Church, Ashington.

He met her when she worked as a barmaid in the Mortimer Working Men's Club (a club around the corner from both Maple Street and Laburnum Terrace).

Initially they have no option after the wedding but to stay with James' parents in Maple Street. This lasts longer than they had first anticipated and the married couple live in one room for a number of years where have two children there before they eventually secure their own home.

England, 1945;

Three years later on 8th of May 1945 saw the end of the Second World War in Europe.

During the war years James' sister Catherine had volunteered to drive ambulances (James continued as a miner, which would become a reserved occupation). In this capacity she meets her future husband Clifford Smith (note 13) and, once they marry they move to Clifford's home tome of Bakewell in Derbyshire where his father runs a sawmill on the banks of the river.

In Clifford's time the family would also run the car park across the bridge and the three daughters of Clifford and Catherine would live in the row of three cottages half way up the hill out of town.

England, 1952;

George the sixth dies in February of this year.

Queen Elizabeth II takes the throne and her coronation takes place on the 2nd of June 1953.

Parkinson

Westminster, London, England, 1957;

A newspaper clipping from Monday 14th October 1957 shows James Parkinson receiving his BEM (British Empire Medal) for services to the mining industry.

He is sixty four years old when he receives his medal from Lord Mills at Lancaster House, Westminster, London.

Jones

Grimsby, England, 1959;

Raymond Jones marries Janet Elizabeth Green on the twelfth of September in Grimsby.

They will relocate to Grimsby and live in the same house throughout their married life from that point.

Reilly

Ashington, Northumberland, England, 1960;
James Reilly has spent his working life at Woodhorn Pit. He will eventually retire in 1972 on ill health grounds at the age of fifty two after thirty four years service. He will receive a certificate for his long service but refuse to display it.

He and Isabella Reilly have a son in January of this year, Edward James, who joins older sisters Isabel, Barbara and Elizabeth to complete their family. They also move to a colliery house soon after their son is born – a two up and two down with no bathroom, an outdoor toilet, and coal fires in every room. The coalhouse was across the road next to the toilet and the tin bath hung on a hook above the dustbin.

Just as the parents of John Reilly before them, Edward's parents held hopes of a better future for their son. One thing that James Reilly was sure of was that his son would not follow in his footsteps and work down the mines.

Ashington, Northumberland, England, 1962;
James Reilly's father, Edward Reilly, dies this year on 10th March aged sixty eight. His wife Elizabeth had died at the end of the previous year, in the 4th quarter of 1961 at Newcastle.

Parkinson

Ashington, Northumberland, England, 1962;
James Parkinson, who retired four years earlier aged sixty five, dies one month after his sixty ninth birthday on the 20th August 1962.
This year, the winter would be the coldest recorded since the start of the industrial revolution.
His wife Frances will continue to 'live in' with her son Leonard, his wife and son. She would reside in the front room while her son and his family lived in the rest of the house.

Jones

Bristol, England, 1964;
On the anniversary of the Queen's coronation, Suzanne Christine Jones is born to parents Raymond and Janet Elizabeth Jones.
Later she will go on marry Edward Reilly and to become Suzanne Christine Reilly.

Reilly

England, 1972;
A strike by miners, which lasts seven weeks, leads to power shortages and a state of emergency is declared by the Heath Government.

Ashington, Northumberland, England, 1976;
James Reilly dies at home on the 20th April 1976 just before his fifty sixth birthday.
Due to the poor health of James, ten days before his death it fell to his son Edward to give away his sister, Elizabeth, at her wedding to James Aston at St. Aidan's church.

Plymouth, Devon, England, 1976;
Later that year Edward James Reilly has joined the Royal Navy and is stationed at Torpoint, Plymouth for two years.
The following summer a young girl called Suzanne Christine Jones coincidentally visits her uncle with her family while the country celebrates the Silver Jubilee of Queen Elizabeth's reign.
Her uncle lives in Plymouth.

The North, England,1984;
A walkout on the 6th March at Cortonwood Colliery leads to the Miners strike which would run to March of the following year.
The hardships that this entailed would affect entire communities and many miners and their families would not have survived without the much needed support of local people running soup kitchens to feed them.
In 1983 Britain had one hundred and seventy four pits – they would all be closed by 2015.

Grimsby, Lincolnshire, England, 1985;
Edward James Reilly and Suzanne Christine Jones meet on a psychiatric ward where he is working as a staff nurse while she is doing her student placement as part of her general nurse training.

Unknown to the male staff on the ward the students in Sue's group have a competition to decide which of the male staff has the best bum.

Sue does not vote for Ed's.

Grimsby, Lincolnshire, England, 1987;
Despite the fact that she hadn't voted for him, Edward James Reilly marries Suzanne Christine Jones in 1987 at St. Giles' Church.

Ashington, Northumberland, England, 1988;
In Ashington the last of its mines closed.

Calverton, Nottinghamshire, England, 1995;
The first colliery that was opened by the National Coal Board (after the end of the second world war all pits were bought by the government and put under the control of the NCB) was in 1952 at Calverton, Nottinghamshire.

Two hundred and two years after the birth of John Reilly in County Cavan, in 1995 Edward and Suzanne's family is completed with the birth of their son, James Edward Reilly who joins his older sisters Lauren and Hannah. The family reside in Calverton at the time.

Calverton colliery was closed by British Coal in 1993.

Ashington, Northumberland, England, 2010;
Isabella Reilly dies on her eighty ninth birthday.

She had previously moved out of the house in Pont Street and taken a council flat in Maple Street, almost opposite the house in which she had started her married life.

Ashington, Northumberland, England, 2017;
The town celebrated its 150th anniversary.

Since 1864 an historic mining celebration has been held annually in Northumberland, only being cancelled during the two World Wars, the General Strike and the miners strikes of 1921 and 1984-85. Originally it was held in Blyth and moved to other locations before being settled in Bedlington for thirty years.

Latterly it has been held in Ashington and Woodhorn.

'The Bedlington Picnic' was a major occasion and thousands would follow the marching colliery bands as they paraded proudly and displayed the intricate colliery banners.

Walesby, Nottinghamshire, England, 2021;
Edward and Suzanne Reilly now live in an ex mining area between the town of Ollerton, where the pit closed in 1995, and Bevercotes, where the mine closed in 1993.

South Yorkshire, England, 2021;
In 1960 there were seventy collieries within a fifteen mile radius of Barnsley. Now there are none. At this time James Reilly (as does his two sisters) lives within a fifteen mile radius of Barnsley.

The UK now imports its coal from as far away as the USA, Russia and Australia.

Notes;

Having fictionalised the events surrounding bare facts of dates, names and addresses the notes provide pointers to where supposition and artistic license have been added to create a more narrative account.

NB. When a place is named as being where someone was born it must be recognised that this would be the registration town not the exact location. Similarly, as the census took place at different times in different years this can explain some age discrepancies.

1. The regiment did march as described but it is mere supposition that they were seen passing the Reilly farm.
2. While this is speculation it seems likely that the regiment did not enjoy the positive regard of the local population.
3. This period of his life has been embellished with a likely scenario surrounding events leading to his marriage.
4. This section provides a fictionalised account of John having a brother Phill. When young James appears later we surmise that this is why he is shown twice on the same census return of two households – once as son and once as nephew.
5. See note 4. This section also provides a fictitious circumstance around how James and his future wife meet.
6. See note 5.
7. When searching through census and other records one often encounters transcription errors which make it difficult to ascertain accurate ages. Similarly, Isabella Parkinson is recorded as being born in 1791 in the 1841 census and in 1789 in that of 1851.
8. See note 4 and note 5. Another piece of artistic license aiming to provide a basis for James and Ann becoming part of the exodus from Ireland.
9. See note 8.

10. It seems likely that the family still work in farming at this point as there is little reason to move to a farm for accommodation when there are pits in nearby towns.

11. It isn't possible to say when the family moved into mining exactly due to the gaps in data, however the period proposed is based on where and when the children were born in Earsdon and not Morpeth. This section also fictionalises how Philip meets and marries.

12. Although Ashington, Pegswood and Morpeth are in relative proximity to each other this section has been fictionalised to provide a possible means of meeting between a miner at Ashington and a girl from Pegswood working at Ashington.

13. No information available to explain how a girl from Ashington meets a man from Derbyshire.

Part Two

The life of Reilly

Two Hundred years of Reilly and Parkinson lineage

Obviously one of the threads woven into the fabric of our family history has been the recurrence of certain names. The table below illustrates this over the generations spanning more than two hundred years;

The Reilly paternal line;
John Reilly b. 1793
James Reilly b. 1827

Philip Reilly b. 1857
Edward Reilly b. 1893
James Reilly b. 1920
Edward James Reilly b. 1960
James Edward Reilly b. 1995

The Reilly maternal line;
Isabella Parkinson b. 1791
Edward Parkinson b. 1835
James Edward Parkinson b.1893
Isabella Parkinson b.1921
Edward James Reilly b. 1960
James Edward Reilly b. 1995

Not to mention;

Great Uncle Jimmy, Uncle Jimmy (another James Edward), Cousin Jimmy…
Isabella Hardy, Great Aunt Isabella, her daughter Isabella, Sister Isabel…
Or the number of times Elizabeth occurs in the various families.

Part Three

The life of Reilly

And now what really happened;

A narrative family history.

Introduction.

They say that the time to ask about family history is while the members are alive. This seems so obvious as to not really require a mention. But I wish that I had done so when I could have done.

I didn't but there is no point having regrets about things one cannot change.

In fairness I did try, even if rather belatedly, while my mam was still alive but I failed to reach further back than my grandparents – and that with very limited success.

So this is an attempt to summarise what I know (as far as I can verify), or can remember (with the inherent discrepancies that process brings) or what I have found out from various family sources. I take full responsibility for any discrepancies, inaccuracies or plain errors. So please be kind; I have done my best.

The majority of the first of these sources of information comes either from original family records (birth certificates, newspaper clippings and other documents) or is supplemented by what input I was able to amass from family members. If unverifiable I have tried to note this as 'according to'. Further information has then been added using a research site allowing transcripts of records and census results to be searched and viewed. The limitation in this method is reached when it is not possible to locate the maiden name of the mother and therefore not possible to search the marriage information of the parents. Also, most of the records there only go back to 1835, but aren't complete for all searches.

The dates and detail such as addresses noted below are therefore factual. The census data is released every ten years, one hundred years later – there are a few more clues in the release of the latest, 1921 data.

A lot of the information on households and jobs comes form searching the 1939 record. This record was made to enable the issue of identity cards and from 1940 used to issue ration books.

The meaning of job roles result from internet searches for definitions.

So this is a family history rather than a tree. In terms of format I am going to itemise couples and then reference to other family members.

Edward James Reilly
May 2021,
Rybeck, Walesby, Nottinghamshire.

1. Edward James Reilly and Suzanne Christine Jones; Ed (me) and Sue.

We met in 1985 on the psychiatric ward at Scartho Road District General Hospital where I worked as a staff nurse and Sue was doing her training placement. I had trained as an RMN (Registered Mental Nurse) up in Northumberland and had some time before I started a conversion course to RGN (Registered General Nurse) in Nottingham so I had chosen a job at Grimsby at random out of the Nursing Times.

We got engaged on 14th Feb 1986 at the Victoria House Restaurant and we married on 23rd May 1987 at St Giles Church, Scartho, Grimsby. Although if the mistake had not been corrected on the marriage certificate we would have been married in 1919! Also, Sue did not live at Derry Way as stated on the certificate; this was her grandmother's address and we used this so that we could be married at the nice old church in Scartho.

We had three Children; Lauren Elizabeth, Hannah Roisin and James Edward.

Our first house was 6 Mickleborough Avenue, Mapperley, Nottingham where we lived from October 1986. I had moved to Nottingham from Grimsby to train as an RGN (Registered General Nurse) and Sue joined me later to train as an RSCN (Registered Sick Children's Nurse). We bought this house for £19,500 and we had to increase the mortgage to £21,000 to have central heating installed. We sold for £41,000. At the time we bought this ridiculously small town house we could have bought a three bed detached nearby for £25,000 but this and consequent price differentials proved beyond our means.

Almost three years later we moved to 27 Hunter Road, Arnold, Nottingham in August 1989. Bought for £58,950 we unfortunately sold for £51,000. Many people at that time found themselves in a phenomenon known as 'negative equity' (basically meaning that your house in most cases was worth less than you paid for it) as this was during a housing market crash.

Lauren was born while we lived here, at Queen's Medical Centre (QMC). Later, Hannah was also born here, but at Nottingham City Hospital.

Next we moved to 37 Broadfields, Calverton, an ex mining town to the north of Nottingham in October 1993. We bought for £79,000 and later sold for £110,000. James was born here, also at Nottingham City Hospital.

We next went further north, to 9 Dalby Croft, Penistone, South Yorkshire from 15th December 2000. This time we bought a new build house, so new that we had no street lights on our cul-de-sac when we moved in. We bought for £129,995 and sold for £315,000.

Then we moved to a bungalow called Rybeck at Forest Lane, Walesby, Newark, Nottinghamshire (Bought for £300,000) from 19th July 2018.

At some point while we lived at Calverton we visited a tourist attraction called 'the World of Robin Hood' – which coincidentally was less than half a mile up the road from Rybeck, toward Bothamsall. Also coincidentally, between selling and moving out of Calverton and before we could move into Penistone we were technically homeless and decided to put everything into storage while we rented a house through a holiday let – in Ollerton (but then remembered that it was actually in nearby Eakring)!

1.1 Edward James Reilly; Me!

I was born 'with a veil over my face' on the 4th January 1960 at 72 Chillingham Crescent, Ashington Northumberland. It was a home birth and I weighed in at 12 lb 4 oz.

I was baptised on the 23rd January 1960 at St. Aidan's Catholic Church, Ashington. My first Holy Communion was on the 25th May 1967.Son of James Reilly and Isabella Parkinson (see 2), my parents moved to 79 Pont Street Ashington sometime in 1960.

Schools;
- St Aidan's Catholic infant and then junior school – both of which were sandwiched between the church and the

graveyard. I passed the '11 plus' selection exam which at that time decided whether you went to a Grammar School or ordinary Secondary School.

- Ashington Grammar School (became Ashington Comprehensive School when the schools system was reformed) until age 16yrs. Really liked maths, not too good at French.

Career;

- Joined the Royal Navy straight from school (10th September 1976 and left 17th March 1980) as a Marine Engineering Artificer (MEA) apprentice at HMS Fisguard in Torpoint, Plymouth. After HMS Fisguard, went up to HMS Caledonia in Rosyth to train as a metalworker and welder; MEA(MW)App. Did not finish the apprenticeship so left not much better off in terms of qualifications or job prospects.
- Not much in the job centre back in Ashington so I applied to do my Registered Mental Nurse training (qualified as a registered mental nurse – RMN – so I have got a certificate stating that I am registered mental, do you have one saying that you are registered sane?) at St Mary's Hospital, Stannington, Morpeth, Northumberland. This was part of the Gateshead School of Nursing. I qualified on the 22nd November 1983. Continued to work at St. Mary's as a Staff Nurse until 29th February 1984. Decided to do conversion to Registered General Nurse (RGN) and decided on Nottingham. In the meantime I decided to work somewhere else rather than stay at St. Mary's.
- Staff Nurse at Scartho Road Hospital in Grimsby from 5th March 1984 (Met Sue during her psychiatric ward placement). Pay was approximately £170 per month in those days.
- Did Registered General Nurse training (RGN) at City Hospital, Nottingham, from 13th May 1985. Sat final exam 24th November 1986.
- Staff Nurse (RMN) at Mapperley Hospital, Nottingham from 29th December 1986.

- Charge Nurse at Coalville Community Hospital, Leicestershire from 14th March 1988. Initially on night shift in charge of the hospital then moving to days in charge of an ESMI 'elderly severe mental illness' ward.
- Nurse Manager at Newstead Hospital then various management posts at Ashfield Hospital, Mansfield Hospital, Newark Hospital all for same Health Authority – North Nottinghamshire HA from 1st April 1991.
- Various management posts when we moved up to Penistone; with Barnsley HA/PCG/PCT, until becoming Assistant Director of Commissioning (commissioning primary care services by contracting with GPs, Pharmacists, Dentists and Opticians) from 30th April 2002 until redundancy during yet another NHS reform and restructuring on the 20th May 2011. Redundancy payments were converted into retirement pension based on almost 31 years NHS service.

If you add the years in the Navy my working life was almost exactly the same as my dad – but not as hard obviously. He received a certificate for long and meritorious service with the national coal board – 34yrs. He refused to put the certificate up on the wall.

After retirement I set up '533 consulting' and did work with various GP practices in Barnsley and Chesterfield for a few years before retiring for good on the 25th August 2016.

Now for some miscellaneous information.

I left school at 16 and most of my academic qualifications came later in life;

- Certificate in Managing Health Services, November 1991, Sheffield City Polytechnic.
- Postgraduate Diploma in Health and Social Services Management, 6th October 1995, Nottingham Trent University.
- MBA awarded 6th March 1998 (Sheffield Hallam University). The graduation ceremony was on the 11th May 1998, The Crucible Theatre, Sheffield. As well as Sue being there, mam and my sisters managed to get there too.

- Diploma in French 31st December 2010 (Open University).
- Certificate in Spanish 31st December 2011(Open University).
- BA (Open) 31st December2012 (Open University).
- TESOL grade A March 2015.

Hobbies;
- Awarded blue belt in judo on the 26th January 1975.
- Summer 1989 became vegetarian at age 29yrs.
- January 1996 became vegan at age 36yrs.
- Reading.
- Cooking strange but usually tasty vegan concoctions.
- Cycling, but more a fair weather cyclist as time went by.
- Gardening.
- Tai chi.
- Studying languages.

Likes and dislikes;
Likes all the family around the table, or on a family/cabin/camping weekend. Likes fine wine, real ale and books around the Napoleonic era.
Really dislikes those little wire ties that Sue puts on food bags.

1.2 Suzanne Christine Jones; Sue!
Sue was born on the 2nd June 1964 at Templemeads Hospital in Bristol. Her parents lived at 4 Longmead Avenue, Bristol, at the time. She was baptised on the 18th October 1964 at Bishopston Methodist Church, Bristol.
Sue's parents were Raymond Jones and Janet Elizabeth Green (see 5). They moved to 96 Brookfield Road, Grimsby in 1967.
Schools;
- Springfield infants then juniors, Grimsby.
- Wintringham secondary school.
- Grimsby College of Technology – Pre nursing course 1980-1982 straight from school.

Career;
- Part time at DB's cash and carry from 16 to 18 yrs old.

- Registered General Nurse training (RGN) at Grimsby School of Nursing 1982-1985. The presentation of Badges and Certificates took place on the 29th October 1986 in the Starlight Room at the Beachcomber Club, Grimsby.
- Worked as a Staff Nurse at Scartho Road Hospital (Paediatrics) 1985-1986. The hospital changed its name to Diana Princess of Wales Hospital later.
- Moved down to Nottingham to undertake her Registered Sick Children's Nurse training (RSCN),1987-1988 based at the Queen's Medical Centre (QMC), Nottingham.
- Staff Nurse after qualifying at QMC, Paediatrics until Dec 2000.
- Staff Nurse at Barnsley DGH from Jan 2001 until 2003 on Paediatrics when we moved up to Penistone from Calverton.
- Various posts in school nursing in Sheffield until retirement (2nd June 2019, aged fifty five) as Practice Teacher/Specialist Community Public Health Nurse.

Now for some miscellaneous information. Her hobbies included;

- Attending Brownies then Guides.
- Being a member of the red cross society (her mum took over the running of the group).
- She passed her cycling proficiency test.
- When younger, enjoyed horse riding and swimming – achieved numerous swimming badges, won a cup for coming 3rd in backstroke.
- Reading.
- Baking.
- Wining and dining.
- Walking and cycling.

Also achieved more academic qualifications later in life;

- ENB 998 Teaching and assessing 1992.

- Health promotion diploma 2003 at Doncaster through Sheffield Hallam University.
- First Class Honours; BA (Hons) Specialist community public health nurse (SCPHN) 2006 Sheffield Hallam University.
- Post Grad Diploma health care education(2009) Practice teacher Sheffield Hallam University.

Likes; Spending time with the family and going away in the caravan (then motorhome) for holidays.

1.3 Lauren Elizabeth Reilly

Lauren was born on the 21st September 1989 at 02:40 a.m. and weighed 7lb 12 oz. She was born at Queens Medical Centre Nottingham. She was christened (CofE) at around 8mths old while we were living at Hunter Road, at St. Mary's Church, Arnold.

Schools;
- Manor Park nursery, Calverton Notts.
- St. Wilfred's CofE primary school, Calverton, Notts.
- Springvale primary school, Penistone S. Yorkshire.
- Penistone Grammar School.
- Huddersfield College – Level 1 and 2 childcare.
- Barnsley college level 3 childcare.

Career;
- Qualified in childcare after four year course.
- Worked in nursery.
- Worked at Asda.
- Special school as a teaching assistant.
- Qualified as paediatric first aider.

Married Ricky Davis, an electrical engineer for Foster's bakery (He gained level 3 NVQ and a level 3 Diploma at Barnsley College), on the 30th June 2012 at Brooklands Hotel, Dodworth.

Ricky was born on the 25th March 1989, (born Ricky Hammil, changed by deed poll on 6th February 1998) at Barnsley hospital, and weighed 6lb 9.5. His parents lived at 42 Hackings Avenue, Cubley at that time (until he was 2 yrs old).

Their children; Tamzin, was born on the 9th September 2013 at Barnsley DGH and Elodie was born on the 4th June 2016 also at Barnsley DGH. Lauren and Ricky lived at 6A Burntwood Road, Grimethorpe at the time.

Lauren really likes Disney and horror.

1.4 Hannah Roisin Reilly

Hannah was born on the 22nd June 1992 at City Hospital Nottingham at 05:04 a.m. and weighed 8lb 12oz.

Schools;

- Manor Park nursery, Calverton Notts.
- St. Wilfred's CofE primary school, Calverton, Notts.
- Springvale primary school, Penistone S. Yorkshire.
- Penistone Grammar School (to 1st year of 6th form).
- (Colouring in course) in Leisure and Tourism at Barnsley College.
- Sheffield Hallam University where she gained a 2:1 in Criminology and Sociology.
- TEFOL.

Career;

- Halfords – Corton Wood.
- Sunglass hut – Meadowhall.
- House of Fraser – Meadowhall.
- Aviva – Sheffield.
- Teaching TESOL in Vietnam.
- Arla – Leeds.
- Teaching.

Met partner Ryan James Byrne, working in Vietnam (or perhaps on the flight there...). Ryan was born on the 10th June 1994 in the National Maternity Hospital. Son of Joseph (then a storeman) and Denise of 34 Connolly Square, Bray, Co. Wicklow, Ireland.

Two children; Lily Ava Byrne was born on the 25th November 2016 and weighed 9lb 9oz, and James Joseph Byrne was born exactly three years later on the 25th November 2019 and weighed 9lb exactly. Both were born at Barnsley Hospital. Their parents lived at 105 Summer Lane at the time.

1.5 James Edward Reilly

James was born on the 2nd February 1995 at City Hospital Nottingham at 13:57 p.m. and weighed 9lb 14 ½ oz; and I have never seen so much blood! Sue was still on the table when I went back that evening to visit.

Schools;
- Manor Park nursery, Calverton Notts.
- St. Wilfred's CofE primary school, Calverton, Notts.
- Springvale primary school, Penistone S. Yorkshire.
- Penistone Grammar School – to six form.
- Decided against completing a degree course at Sheffield Hallam University (twice).

Career;
- McDonalds. (09/2013-12/2019) 3 years as a Shift Manager, First 4 years in Meadowhall, the last 2 in Leeds Kirkstall.
- KDA warehouse Dodworth Barnsley from 03/2021.
- Amazon

Miscellaneous information;
- Brown belt karate.
- Likes to travel.
- Enjoys games, films and quizzes.
- Enjoys ales.
- Enjoys reading, especially Game of Thrones and Terry Pratchett.
- Went to Malaysia while at 6th Form – World Challenge.
- Went inter-railing in Europe, (Brussels, Bruges, Amsterdam, Berlin, Prague, Krakow, Ljubljana, Budapest, Florence, Rome) Summer 2016.
- Went to Vietnam Summer 2017.
- On 12/01/2020 he set off to Asia and then Thailand for a years travels in New Zealand; just in time for COVID lockdown/restrictions.

Lived at;

- 384 Ecclesall Road S1 8PJ (01/07/2014 – 31/06/2016), Sheffield.
- 21 Cutlery Works S3 7BG (30/08/2016 – 31/07/2017) – Sheffield.
- 4 Severn Road S10 2SU (31/10/2017 – 30/07/2018) – Leed.
- 29 Foxcroft Mount LS6 3NN (16/06/2018 – 15/12/2019) - Leeds

2 James Reilly and Isabella Parkinson; Ed's parents
Married; 3rd December 1942, St. Aidan's Catholic Church, Ashington.
Four children; Isabel, Barbara, Elizabeth, Edward James (see 1.1)
Shared a house with Nana Reilly (at 93 Maple Street; the house was almost opposite the flat that mam moved into later) before moving to 72 Chillingham Crescent, Ashington Northumberland.
Moved to 79 Pont Street Ashington in 1960. Two up and two down, no bathroom, outdoor toilet, coal fires (coalhouse across the road next to the toilet).

2.1 James Reilly (dad)
'Jimmy' (dad) was born on the 28th June 1920. He died at home on the 20th April 1976 aged 55yrs from cerebral and renal metastases from bronchogenic carcinoma.
Lived at;
- 9 Katherine Street Ashington
- 93 Maple Street Ashington
- 72 Chillingham Crescent Ashington
- 79 Pont Street Ashington

Worked at Woodhorn Colliery for 34 years (colliery timber drawer/miner) from the age of 18 before ill health retirement at age 52. Had to stop working down the pit in 1968; his last day working there was the 28th of March. He then had over a year of operations and physio due to cartilage trouble. Had all cartilages removed and as part of physio learned how to swim late in life. Also was convinced that he saw the 'ghost of the white lady' when at the convalescent home near Morpeth.
Went back to light work on the 6th of January 1969 but was unable to continue after one day as he jerked his right leg. He was then off sick until he finished on Saturday the 16th of January 1970 but had his service reckoned to 1972.
After that he tried to find a job; didn't last as a school caretaker but did a couple of years working at Draeger-Normalair over at Bedlington making safety masks (Mask Visor Operator).
Son of Edward Reilly and Elizabeth Nicholson Smith.

Liked Christmas – dancing to Crackling Rosie, drinking whisky and black, and smoking Tom Thumb cigars.
Liked to bet on horses and watch sport. Taught me to play snooker at the age of 11.

2.2 Isabella Parkinson

'Belle' (mam) was born on the 23rd August 1921 Cornforth, Sedgefield (a short distance from Ferryhill). She received her first Holy Communion in 1932 at St. Aidan's Church, Ashington. Died 23rd August 2010 in Ashington hospital following a fall at home. She died on her birthday.
She met dad when she was a barmaid at the Mortimer Working Men's Club.
The funeral took place at St. Aidan's on Friday the 3rd of September followed by cremation at Cowpen Crematorium.
Lived at;

- Chilton nr Ferryhill Durham. Christened Catholic at Sedgefield.
- 39 Laburnham Terrace Ashington
- 93 Maple Street Ashington, from June 1943
- 72 Chillingham Crescent Ashington
- 79 Pont Street Ashington
- 70 Sycamore Street Ashington

To explain why 70 Sycamore is opposite 93 Maple – the street names refer to the narrow garden area at the front of the houses while the actual road/street is technically the back of the houses where they face the other street.
First Holy Communion, St. Aidan's Church, Ashington, on the feast of the Immaculate Conception 1932
Daughter of James Parkinson and Frances Hardy (see 3)
Had four children; Isobel, Barbara, Elizabeth and Edward James
Liked dancing (usually with Aunty Alice)
Heinz tomato soup was the usual cure for any illness.

2.3 Isabel Reilly

Isabel was born on the 19th August 1948.

She was married to Douglas Johnson on 3rd December 1964 (later divorced).

Dougie, a plant operator, was born on the 21st June 1941.

They had three children; Ailsa (A factory worker, was born on the 8th April 1966. She married Alan Wills, a security guard, who was born on the 20th May 1964. The wedding took place on the 5th October 1984), Hepson (A mechanic, was born on the 9th January 1968 – he later moved to Germany to live and work as a refuse collector) and Hayley (an office worker who was born on the 6th February 1973).

Isabel then married David Wallace (who was born on the 10th November 1948) on 10th November 1984 (later divorced). Dave had worked in steelwork, colliery and as a publican.

Isabel mainly worked as a publican.

Latterly lived with John, her partner in 8th Row, Ashington before moving into a retirement complex (built on the site of the old Ashington Hospital)

2.4 Barbara Reilly

DOB 23rd February 1952

Worked as barmaid and later as Carer for Age Concern.

Married Alan Twist – divorced.

Had two children; Deborah (DOB 13th August 1972, married Michael Oliver) and Nichola (DOB 3rd July 1975).

Married Steven Rees – divorced.

Married Gary Wendt (taxi driver).

Lives at 22 Bamburgh Terrace – not too far from Chillingham Crescent.

2.5 Elizabeth Reilly

Liz was born on the 5th June 1956; died of breast cancer/secondaries on the 21st December 1999 aged 43yrs.

After school she worked in a clerical post at the fire station at Morpeth before serving as a Leading Wren (Writer), Royal Navy for 4 ½ years (based at RNAS Culdrose at Helston in Cornwall). After that she worked as a P.A. Wincanton Logistics and then P.A. to School headmaster.

She was married to James Aston, who was born on the 26th July 1955 (later they divorced). The marriage took place on 10th April 1976 at St. Aidan's Church, Ashington. I gave her away as dad was too ill (he died 10 days later).

Jim was born in Manchester. He joined the Royal Navy as an Artificer apprentice before transferring and retraining to eventually become a CPO (Aircraft Mechanic) Royal Navy. During his service he was awarded the Northern Island medal and the Gulf medal.

Two children; Martina (DOB 20th December 1978, graduated Nottingham University 2000) and Stephanie (DOB 29th March 1981). Spent last years at Ditcheat with her partner Roger Yeoman.

2.6 Edward James Reilly
(see 1.1)

3 Edward Reilly and Elizabeth Nicholson Smith; Ed's paternal grandparents

The information in 3.1 and 3.2 below is as reliable as can be reasonably expected. Using records available from various census collections a likely family lineage has been constructed with reasonable levels of confidence based on logical assumptions and is shown at 3.5.

3.1 Edward Reilly (Grandad)

Edward Reilly (granddad)was born on the 5th of April 1893 according to the 1939 register. He died on the 10th March 1962. His year of birth on the death entry is 1894.

He worked as a Colliery Stoneman (Below) at Woodhorn Colliery Ashington. A stoneman was a worker who dealt with stone or rock rather than coal and usually meant someone who worked on the development of a stone drivage. A drivage was a new gate road leading to the face.

He married Elizabeth Nicholson Smith in August 1917.

In the 1939 register his household was at 93 Maple Street, Ashington;

- Edward Reilly (granddad), 05 Apr 1893 (not 1894),Colliery stoneman below

- Elizabeth N. Reilly, 07 July 1895, Unpaid domestic duties

- Catherine A. Reilly, 20 June 1912 (more accurate source, 20 June 1917), Unpaid domestic duties

- James Reilly (dad), 28 June 1920, Colliery putter below

- James Smith (boarder) – uncle Jimmy Smith, 6 Dec 1908,Colliery shift worker below

In the 1911 census, Edward Reilly (1894 not 1893), is at Seghill, Tynemouth, son of Philip and Catherine Reilly.

1911 Reilly household, of New Square, Seghill, consisted of;

- Philip Reilly (great grandad), 1857, 54 yrs old, Coal miner Hewer, Embleton

- Catherine Reilly, 1858, 53 yrs old, Houghton, Durham

- John Reilly, 1888, 23yrs old, Coal miner hewer, Seaton Delaval

- Edward Reilly (granddad),1894 (not 1893), 17 yrs old, Coal miner siding rope boy, Seaton Delaval

- Mary Reilly, 1896, 15 yrs old, Seaton Delaval

- Joseph Reilly, 1889, 13 yrs old, Coal miner Driver, Seaton Delaval

- Anthony Mullarkey (boarder), 1889, 22 yrs old, Coal miner hewer, Mayo, Ireland

I am confident of this being granddad despite the date discrepancy as I am aware of this side of the family being in Ashington later. This would make Philip Reilly (1857) my great granddad.

3.1.1 Philip Reilly (1857); Ed's great granddad.
The 1939 register shows Philip Reilly, born 17 August 1857, coal miner (retired), widowed, living at St. Josephs House, Westmorland Road, Newcastle.
In the 1911 census Philip's household is in Seaton Delaval. To give an idea of proximity; Seghill is less than 2 miles from Seaton Delaval.
While his oldest son, also Philip (1882) does not show up in the 1911 household above he does appear in the 1901 census. This shows Philip (1882) as being the older brother of Edward Reilly (1894/1893)

The Reilly household in 1901, at 8 Rouble Row, New Hartley, Seaton Delaval, consists of;

- Philip Reilly (great grandad),1857 44yrs old, Coal miner hewer, Embleton

- Catherine Reilly, 1858, 43 yrs old, Rainton, Durham

- Philip Reilly, 1882, 19 yrs old, Coal miner putter below ground, Earsdon

- Catherine Reilly, 1884, 17 yrs old, Earsdon

- James Reilly, 1886, 15 yrs old, Coal miner sheave lad below ground, Earsdon

- John Reilly, 1888, 13 years old, Coal miner driver below ground, Earsdon

- Edward Reilly (granddad), 1894, 7 yrs old, Earsdon

- Mary Reilly, 1896, 5 yrs old, Earsdon

- Joseph Reilly, 1898, 3 yrs old, Earsdon

And again, if we look at the 1891 census for the same Reilly household – then at Camp Terrace, Seaton Delaval, Tynemouth, it shows;

- Philip Reilly (great grandad), 1857, 34 yrs old, Coal miner, Embleton

- Catherine Reilly, 1858, 33 yrs old, Houghton

- Philip Reilly, 1883 (not 1882 as above), 8 yrs old, Scholar, Earsdon

- Catherine, 1884, 7 yrs old, Scholar, Earsdon

- James, 1886, 5 yrs old, Scholar, Earsdon

- John Reilly, 1888, 3 yrs old, Scholar, Earsdon

- James Duffy (f-in-law), 1834, 57 yrs old, Coal miner, Ireland

This provides a further example of how recorded dates/ages can vary from one census to another and of course due to subsequent transcription error.

Of note; John Reilly would go on to join the army in the First World War as Private 4630 Reilly J. Northumberland Fusiliers. It appears that they landed in France in May 1915. John died aged 27 on the 26th November 1915. In the record set; Commonwealth War Graves Commission Debt of Honour his grave reference is; F. 10. Ashington (St. Aidan's) Roman Catholic Cemetery, Husband of Susan Brown (formerly Reilly) of 55 Katherine Street, Ashington.

In the ten years to 1901, Philip and Catherine, the two oldest have left to set up their own households. The 1911 census shows Philip's household at 49 Sycamore St., Hirst, Ashington;

- Philip Reilly (granddad's older brother), 1882 (not 1883), Coal hewer, New Hartley

- Ellen Reilly, 1892, Amble

- Catherine Reilly, 1911,New Hirst

The 1939 register shows the youngest brother, Joseph, having a household at 67 Katherine Street, Ashington, and consisting of;

- Joseph Reilly (granddad's younger brother), 02 Aug 1897 (not 1898), Deputy, Overman below, heavy worker

- Catherine Reilly, 03 Sept 1898, Unpaid domestic duties

- Philip Reilly, 12 Jul 1921, General Hotel Porter, heavy worker

- Desmond Reilly, 03 Apr 1924, Shop assistant, grocery

- Kathleen Reilly, 19 Jul 1934, At school

3.1.2 James Reilly; Ed's great great granddad

The 1861 census of the Reilly household, at Tritlington North Farm, Tritlington Holms, Tritlington, Morpeth, consists of;

- James Reilly (Ed's great great granddad),1827,Labourer, Ireland

- Ann Reilly, 1833, Ireland

- Mary Reilly, 1855,Durham

- Philip Reilly (Ed's great granddad),1857, Embleton

- Margaret Reilly,1859,Embleton

- James Reilly, 1861, Hebron Northumberland

- Thomas Smith (boarder),1830, Ireland

- Mary Smith (boarder),1838, Ireland

- Mary Smith (boarder),1857, Embleton

- Ellen Smith,1861, Embleton

The Embleton noted above is in Durham near Sedgefield.

In the 1891 census we have the Reilly household at Quarry Row, Seaton Delaval;

- James Reilly (great great granddad), 1827, Retired coal miner, Ireland

- Ann Reilly, 1834 (or 1833 in 1861 census), Ireland

- Catherine Reilly, 1869, Morpeth

- Hugh Reilly, 1877, Coal miner driver, Earsdon

- Edward James Reilly (grandson), 1887, Earsdon

- John Reilly (boarder), 1869, Coal miner, Gateshead

Philip (1857) had left home by now as he was 34 yrs old and had his own household at Seaton Delaval (see above). Philip Reilly (1857) married Catherine Duffy in the 3rd quarter of 1879, at Chester le Street, Durham. This fits with Catherine being from Houghton le Spring, Durham.

There is evidence that James Reilly (1827) married Ann Wilson in Bailieborough, County Cavan in 1853 – this fits with them being Irish and also with moving to England and having the eldest child, Mary in 1855 in Durham.

This would mean that they emigrated between 1853 and 1855. He is recorded as a labourer so perhaps a farm labourer given his father was a farmer? He obviously moved into mining at a later date.

To give an idea of proximity; Ashington is 12 miles north of Seghill, Seghill is less than 2 miles from Seaton Delaval. New Hartley is a couple of miles from Seaton Delaval. Rainton is about three miles from Houghton le Spring. Earsdon is a few miles south of Seaton Delaval on the outskirts of Newcastle. Tritlington is near Morpeth. Durham is about 8 miles from Houghton le Spring.

Tracing James Reilly back to Ireland is a little difficult. From the 1841 Ireland census it is known that he was 14 years old and not at school but could read.

Of the two James Reilly's born 1827 in County Cavan (where he later married) it seems likely that he is part of one of the two Reilly households recorded below, from the 1841 Ireland census;

Philip Reilly's household – all persons shown as being at Townland; Coradownan, Parish; Killashandra, Barony; Tullyhunco, County; Cavan;

- Phill Reilly (a farmer), 30, 1811

- Bridget Reilly, 30, 1811

- Patt Reilly, 6, 1835

- Catherine Reilly, 4, 1837

- Anne Reilly, 2, 1839

- Bridget, 1, 1840

- James (nephew) – great great granddad?, 14, 1827

The other (I believe more likely) is as above but at Corr, not Coradownan;

- John Reilly, 48, 1793

- Elizabeth Reilly, 56, 1785

- Catherine Reilly, 16, 1825

- James Reilly – great great granddad?, 14, 1827

- John Reilly, 11, 1830

Corr is less than 10 miles from Coradownan. In fact, given the inconsistency of recording they could both be the same James Reilly and Phil could be a younger brother of John – who knows!

3.2 Elizabeth Nicholson Smith (Ed's grandma)
Was born on the 7th July 1895 according to the 1939 register. Had two children; Catherine Anne and James.
She was baptised 6/8/1885 at Morpeth. Died in the 4th quarter of 1961 at Newcastle.

3.3 Catherine Ann Reilly
Was born 20th June 1917 (Died 14th February 1961). which if accurate means she was born before her parents married in August that year.
Driver in the ATS during the war. Presumably this is how she met her future husband as there doesn't seem to be any other connection between Ashington and Bakewell.

Married 1st September 1945 at All Saints, Bakewell to Clifford Hudson Smith (DOB 11th April 1923) who owned a saw mill at Bakewell, Derbyshire and later the Car park next to the bridge in Bakewell. Clifford died on the 11th June 1994.

According to the 1939 register the Smith household was at Rutland Works, Bakewell and consisted of;
- George F. Smith, born 9/4/1885, an English and Foreign timber merchant, saw miller, contractor and undertaker
- Mary Smith who was born on 24th July 1897.
- Clifford H. Smith, born 11 April 1923, an English Timber merchant and saw miller, Managing Assistant.
- Barbara Smith, a school teacher, born 26 June 1920.

They lived at Rutland Works, Bakewell.
Catherine and Clifford had three daughters; Patricia May, born on the 8th of March 1947, Sheila Elizabeth, born on the 9th of May 1948 and Muriel Evelyn who was born on the 16th of February 1950.

3.3.1 Patricia May Smith
DOB 8th March 1947
Married Robin Hooten and had one son Andrew Hooten

3.3.2 Sheila Elizabeth Smith
DOB 9th May 1948
Married Michael Briggs, then John Francis Power, then David Albert Whitaker.
No children.

3.3.3 Muriel Evelyn Smith
DOB 16th February 1950
Married David William Rhodes on 30th June 1973, a works foreman for the local council.
Had two children; Philip David Rhodes, (DOB 23rd April 1980) and James Stephen Rhodes (DOB 17th September 1981)

3.4 James Reilly
(see 2.1)

4 James (Edward) Parkinson and Frances Hardy; Ed's maternal grandparents

4.1 James (Edward) Parkinson
Not clear if his name was just James Parkinson. It is James Edward on the marriage certificate of mam and dad but on his service record and 'mentioned in dispatches', as well as the 1939 register he is only recorded as James Parkinson.

At that time the household was at 39 Laburnum Terrace. Ashington;
- James Reilly, born 6 July 1893, a Colliery Conveyor Drawer
- Frances Parkinson, born 7 July 1893, unpaid domestic duties
- Edward P. Parkinson (single), born 17 Sep 1883, Colliery boiler fireman heavy
- Alice Burt, born 6 Feb 1920, unemployed
- Isabella Reilly (mam), born 28/8/1921, unpaid domestic duties.

He was born on the 7th July 1893 in the county of Durham.
Not sure who Edward P. above is. Also, the use of Burt and Reilly, both married names, is probably due to the original register being updated and annotated.
A newspaper clipping from Monday 14th October 1957 shows that James received his BEM (British Empire Medal for services to the mining industry) at the age of 64 from Lord Mills at Lancaster House, Westminster, London. The clipping also states that;
He worked in the pits from age 13, Sherburn Hill Colliery, Durham. Also worked in Mainsforth, Durham, then Scremerston, near Berwick. Started at Ashington 1910 or 1911 before working at Morpeth Moor, joined the Army in 1911, joined up with the Gordon Highlanders (among the first 100,000 to fight in the 1914-18 war). Mentioned in dispatches. Had one of his lungs shot out in the war. Private 745 Gordon Highlanders.Returned to Ashington – Ellington Colliery, but called up again in 1921 because of the Miners Strike. After release from the Army went to Linton Colliery for the rest of his working life. Suffered spinal injury, held various posts after that.

Was a timber drawer at one point. He was also a former chairman of Linton branch of the National Union of Mineworkers
James retired aged 65 and died on the 20th August 1962.

It appears that his father (Ed's great grandfather) was called Edward Parkinson (1837). The 1901 census records the household, at Pontop House, East Rainton, Houghton le Spring, Durham as the following;

- Edward Parkinson, 64 yrs old, born 1837 (not 1835 as will be seen), Coal Miner
- Barbara Parkinson, 34 yrs old, born 1867, Consett, Durham, (wife)
- James Parkinson (Ed's granddad), 8 yrs old, born 1893, Durham
- Alice A. Smith (visitor), 18 yrs old, born 1883, Sunnyside, Durham.

Barbara was a second wife but her maiden name was Mellon, so presumably Alice is a relative by her previous marriage, possibly her sister in law or feasibly her daughter. The wedding record records Edward marrying Ellen Smith in the third quarter of 1892, recorded at Sunderland. Her full name was Barbara Ellen Smith.

The 1891 census shows Edward married previously, then living at North Pit, East Rainton, Houghton le Spring, Durham;

- Edward Parkinson, 56 yrs, born 1835 (not 1837), coal miner, born England
- Anne Parkinson (wife), 46 yrs old, born 1845, London.

Anne died in the third quarter of 1891 Houghton le Spring.
The 1881 census shows him and Anne at the same location. The 1871 census shows him at the same location but not married;

- Edward Parkinson, 36 yrs, born 1835, Durham
- Philip Todd (nephew), 20 yrs, born 1851, Durham
- Isabella Parkinson (niece), 23 yrs, born 1848, Durham
- William Parkinson (niece's son), 1 yr, 1870, Durham.

The 1861 census, curiously, reports the household at Seaham Road, Houghton le Spring, Durham;

- Edward Parkinson, 26 yrs, born 1835, Coal miner, born West Rainton, Durham
- Isabella Parkinson (sister), 13 yrs, born 1848, Durham
- James William Parkinson (brother), 2 yrs, born 1859, Durham.

The 1851 census has the household at Market Place, Houghton le Spring, Durham;

- Isabella Rawling (widow), 62 yrs, born 1789, Felling, Durham
- Elizabeth Rawling (married), 21 yrs, born 1830, Durham
- Isabella Parkinson (unmarried), 19 yrs, 1832, Durham
- Edward A. Parkinson (great grandad of Ed), 16 yrs, born 1835, coal miner, Durham
- Isabella Parkinson (granddaughter), 3 yrs, born 1848, Durham
- Margaret Ann Parkinson 0 yrs, 1851.

In 1841 the census records the household at Rainton West, Houghton le Spring, Durham, England;

- Isabella Parkinson, 50 yrs, 1791 (not 1789 as above), Durham
- William Parkinson, 20 yrs, born 1821, Durham
- John Parkinson, 15 yrs, 1826, Durham; Elizabeth Parkinson, 6yrs, born 1835, Durham
- Isabella Parkinson, 5 yrs, born 1836, Durham
- Edward Parkinson, 6 yrs, born 1835, Durham.

Isabella Parkinson married Edward Rawling in the 3rd quarter of 1841.

The 1911 census shows Barbara Ellen re-married in the 4th quarter of 1906, presumably after the death of Edward Parkinson. She was now at 10 Edward Street, Morpeth;

- John Allen, 65 yrs old, 1846, Stone miner in coal mine, born at Jarrow, Durham

- Ellen Allen, 43 years old, 1868 (not 1867), Consett, Durham
- Joseph Allan, 4 yrs old, 1907, East Howle, Ferry Hill, Durham
- James Parkinson (step son), 17 yrs old, 1894 (not 1893), Coal miner, hand putter above ground, born North Pit, Hetton, Durham.

Hetton is 2 miles from Houghton.

4.2 Frances Hardy (Ed's nana Parky)
Was born on the 6th (or 7th) July 1893 (died 10th January 1976).
Married James in August 1916. Daughter of Ralph Hardy (a band master from Pegswood) and Isabella (unknown surname).Had four children; James Edward, Alice, Isabella and Leonard Bruce.

1901 census Hardy household, 63 Clyde Street, Hurst, Morpeth.;

- Ralph Hardy, 28, 1873, Coal Miner, Bothal

- Isabella Hardy, 26, 1875, Bothal

- Frances Hardy (nana), 7, 1894 (not 1893), Bothal

- Deborah Hardy, 5, 1896, Woodhorn

- Isabella Hardy, 1, 1900, Woodhorn

By 1911 she no longer shows in the Hardy household at 197 Longhirst Terrace, Pegswood, Morpeth;

- Ralph Hardy, 38, 1873, Coal Miner Hewer, Ashington

- Isabella Hardy, 36, 1875, Ashington

- Deborah Hardy, 15, 1896,Hirst

- Isabella Hardy, 11, 1900, Hirst

- Thomas Hardy, 8, 1903, Hirst

- Mary Jane Hardy, 7, 1904, Radcliffe

- Florance Hardy, 2, 1909, Pegswood

- Margaret Ann Hardy, 1, 1910, Pegswood

But she shows up in the Baird Household, 43 Third Row, Ashington;

- Richard Baird, 46, 1865, Coal Miner Deputy, Bedlington

- Phillis Baird, 44, 1867, Choppington

- John Baird, 24, 1887, Coal Miner Rolley-Way Man, Choppington

- Alexander Baird, 22, 1889, Cambois

- Thomas Baird, 20, 1891, Stakeford

- Edward Baird, 19, 1892, Stakeford

- Frances Hardy (servant), 18, 1893, Ashington

Frances was reputedly one of thirteen children. Ralph Hardy appears in the 1939 register with the following details;
Born 09 Jan 1873, Retired Miner (widowed). He is registered as living at 13 Pelaw Crescent, Chester le Street Durham in the household of his married daughter Deborah, now Burrell, DOB 14 May 1895 (not 1896).

4.3 James Edward Parkinson
Was born on the 17th September 1917 and died on the 6th July 1988.
Interests; Amateur boxer.
Worked at Linton Colliery as Electric Winder, presumably this was in connection with the winding gear used to bring coal up, men up and down, and machinery down.
Owned his own house at a time when every other family member in Ashington had either a council house or colliery house.
Engineer in the war and fought up through Italy to Ypres.

Married Mary Doris Dodd (DOB 21st November 1922) in the second quarter of 1956.
No children.

4.4 Alice Parkinson

DOB 6th February 1920 (died 1st October 1994)

Married Andrew Short (DOB 12th November 1907, died 10th March 1962 – Was at Dunkirk in the Army, worked at Linton Colliery)

Two children; Judith (DOB 14th November 1943, married 5th December 1959 to John Coxon DOB 13th March 1932; had four children, Angela DOB 16th July 1964, Heather DOB 20th October 1966, Steven DOB 3rd July 1969, and Colin DOB 15th October 1976) and James Edward Short (DOB 9th May 1950).

Married Evan Burt on 2nd November 1963 (DOB 3rd March 1922, died 6th July 1988; worked as electrician at Ashington Colliery)

Anecdotally Aunty Alice worked 'in service' at Chillingham Castle.

4.5 Isabella Parkinson

(see 2.2)

4.6 Leonard Bruce Parkinson

DOB 13th December 1933

Married Mary Gertrude Brady (DOB 8th May 1934)

One child; Gary Leonard, DOB 31st December 1959 – died in his sleep on the 27th February 2003, aged 43 yrs from a brain haemorrhage; Married Tracy Victoria Hamilton on the 22nd July 1989. They had one child, Zaxon Levi.

5 Raymond Jones and Janet Elizabeth Green; Sue's parents
Lived at 96 Brookfield Road, Scartho, Grimsby from 1967 until Janet's death in 2017.
Had two children Karen Margaret and Suzanne Christine.

5.1 Raymond Jones
Born a twin (Brother Bill lived in London – see 6.2). Born in Princes Street, Bristol, DOB 25th March 1933, died 11th February 2021 in the Grove Care Home. Cremated at Grimsby Crematorium 23rd February 2021, of old age and skin cancer (despite also having every condition you could possibly name!)
Married Janet Elizabeth Green (DOB 27th January 1937), at St James' Church Grimsby on 12th September 1959. According to the marriage certificates their ages were both recorded incorrectly!
Son of Charles Henry Jones (DOB 22nd December 1897, died 14th July 1964) and Elsie May Pugsley (DOB 15th March 1899 at Bedminster, Bristol, died 1st March 1978) (see 6).
He left school at age 14yr and did various factory jobs until he later signed up for three years in the RAF. He was stationed at Yatesbury and trained as a telex operator.
Worked most of his life as an office worker/manager in Raynor's electrical shop in Grimsby until retirement. Was a wages clerk at a builders at the time Sue was born.
Following Janet's death he had to move into the Grove Care Home at Waltham where he spent three and a half years.

5.2 Janet Elizabeth Jones
Janet was born on the 27th January 1937 and died on the 10th August 2017 (St Andrews Hospice Grimsby – cremated at Grimsby Crematorium 17th August 2017) of bowel & liver cancer.
Daughter of Jack Wilyman Green (DOB 1st April 1909, died 4th June 1974 of Coronary Thrombosis) and Beatrice 'Beaty' Frances Hopper (DOB 12th August 1909, died 9th October 1995 – Beatrice later married Jack Lakeman when she was over 80 yrs old, at St Giles Scartho) (see 7).

She attended nursery, infant and junior school at South Parade, near the General Hospital, before going on to attend Armstrong Secondary Modern and then Grimsby College of Further Education.

Lived at 44 Phyllis Avenue Grimsby then, when they moved back to Grimsby from Bristol (in 1968), at 96 Brookfield Road.

She worked as a nurse, starting pre nursing at 16 ½ at Sheffield Royal Hospital. She then progressed to train at the same hospital to become an SRN (training Jan 1955 to April 1958 – registered 31st March 1958). she met Ray just before her final exams while on holiday at Paignton.

She worked in two hospitals in Bristol; Southmead Hospital, Homeopathic Hospital, then returned to Southmead Hospital, between May 1958 and May 1967 during which time she completed part one midwifery. She took time out between 1962 and 1966 when Karen and Sue were born.

Various nursing posts followed her return to Grimsby; initially working at Springfield Hospital then moving to Scartho Road Hospital until retirement as a Theatre Recovery Sister at age 61 on 31st March 1998. After that she spent the next 13 years as a volunteer doing massage and nails for the elderly.

She served as Grimsby youth officer for the British Red Cross for over 20 yrs. In recognition of her service she was awarded life membership of the British Red Cross Society in April1987.

Got engaged at Bristol zoo.

5.3 Karen Margaret Jones
DOB 25th April 1962 at Bristol.
Qualified as State Enrolled Nurse at Grimsby.
Moved to America, married Richard Wohlers.
Worked in Health Insurance before setting up as a photographer.
Had two children Nicholas and Alex.
Richard already had a child, Tony, when he and Karen met (Tony married Racquel and had three children, Anthony, Isabella and Evelyn). Richard was a house builder.

5.4 Suzanne Christine Jones
(See 1.2)

6 Charles Henry Jones and Elsie May Pugsley; Sue's paternal grandparents

Elsie May Pugsley was born in Bedminster, Bristol

She married Charles Henry Jones, in the first quarter of 1931 and they had twins; Raymond and William DOB 25th March 1933.

They lived at Princes Street at the time of their births but later moved to 20 Alfred Street, Bristol.

The 1911 census shows the Jones family at 3 Burton Court, Clifton, Bristol. Charles mother is recorded as head of the family;

- Rosina Jones (widow), born 1874
- Charles Henry Jones, born 1897 (not 1896 as later recorded)
- Alice Jones, born 1902
- Sidney Jones, born 1904
- Frederick Jones, born 1906.

In the 1939 register the Jones family resides at Princes Street;

- Charles Henry Jones, born 22 Nov 1896, General Labourer
- Elsie May Jones, born 15 Nov 1899, unpaid domestic duties
- and three officially closed entries, two of which will be Bill and Ray.

6.1 Raymond Jones
See 5.1

6.2 William Jones
DOB 25th March 1933
Painter and decorator, lived in Hornchurch.
Married Irene Walker (died 14 November 2020 in her sleep).
Had three children; Catherine, Sarah and Matthew.

6.2.1 Catherine Jones
Married John Barber.
Had two children; Jessica (DOB 18th April 1989) and Hannah (DOB 2nd May 1990)

6.2.2 Sarah Jones
DOB 6th April 1965.
Married Andrew Cansell.
Lived in Hornchurch.
Had two children; Daniel and Bethany.

6.2.3 Matthew Jones
Married Sue, had two children; Emma and Laura.
Moved up to live and work in Chesterfield.

7 Jack Wilyman Green and Beatrice Frances Hopper; Sue's maternal grandparents

Beatrice was the youngest of six children. Born in Grimsby on 12th August 1909.

Beaty married Jack Wilyman Green (who was born on the 1st April 1909 and died on the 4th June 1974 of Coronary Thrombosis while they were on holiday celebrating his retirement at Ayr – the body had to be transported back for the funeral).

The wedding took place on the 16th June 1934 at the Parish Church Grimsby. Jack was baptised Primitive Methodist on 23rd April 1909. Jack lost one of his eyes. He worked as a baker at the time they were married and then as a British Railway Lengthman/Trackman.

A lengthman looked after a length of track and dealt with minor issues as they arose. These could range from ensuring that any tracks that had worked loose were hammered back into place to dealing with drainage and subsidence. If a major problem was found he would ensure that the trains were stopped from running.

Sue's grandparents lived at;

- 44 Phyllis Avenue Grimsby.
- 15 St. Augustine Avenue Grimsby.

A completion statement dated the 8th March 1985 shows that Beaty sold the property at St. Augustine way for £11,950, leaving her a balance of £11,531.15.

They had three children; Janet Elizabeth, Byron John and Carol Ann. Later Beaty married another Jack (Lakeman) at St. Giles on Saturday the 12th of September 1992. They lived at 25 Derry Way Grimsby; Beaty's home following the sale of the propety at St. Augustine.

Sue's maternal great-grandparents; Beaty's parents were Alfred Earnest Hopper (DOB 29th September 1871, died 25th August 1962 aged 90 yrs in Edgeware General Hospital, Hendon – presumably had been living with his daughter Clara Wadkin of 56 Elsmleigh Avenue Kenton. He died of congestive cardiac failure and bilateral gangrene of feet), a tradesman, fish merchant (fish offal buyer) and dock hand. He married Annie Elizabeth Wood on the 4th December

1897 (DOB 4th December 1897, died 26th February 1930 aged 59 from a cerebral haemorrhage) at St Andrews Church Grimsby and lived at 42 Cleethorpes Road. Alfred only had one eye.

Annie's father was George Wood (deceased at the time of the marriage). Alfred and Ann lived at 10 Peppercorn Walk Grimsby.

Sue's maternal great-great-grandparents; The parents of Alfred Earnest Hopper were George Hopper, a shipwright, and Clara Alice Lowery. A shipwright is someone who builds or does carpentry concerned with wooden vessels.

George was born at Louth in 1844 and (unconfirmed) died in 1925. Clara was born in the second quarter of 1848, Caistor, Lincolnshire. No record found of her death date. They married in the third quarter of 1879, Caistor.

They lived at King Edward Street North, Grimsby at the time Alfred was born.

Clara's parents were Thomas Lowery born 1826 (unconfirmed), of Swinhop St, Swinhope, Caistor. He married Ann Woolsey at Caistor in the fourth quarter of 1844.

Sue's paternal great-grandparents; Jack's parents were Silas Green, a carpenter and Wheelwright (Journeyman) and Jane Kate Wilyman. A journeyman is someone who has successfully completed an official apprenticeship qualification and is considered competent and authorized to work as a fully qualified employee. A wheelwright is a craftsman that makes and repairs wooden wheels.

Silas was born in the 2nd quarter of 1869 at Louth and died in the 3rd quarter of 1928. He and Jane married in the 4th quarter of 1896 at Spilsby, Lincs. Jane was born in the 3rd quarter of 1873, Spilsby, but there is no record of her death.

At the time of Jack's birth they lived at 25, College Street Cleethorpes.

Jack's sister, Janet's aunty Mary; Evelyn Mary Green, according to the death certificate died 16th October 1980 and was 'said to be born on' 19th November 1900 (actually born on 26th November 1900 according to the birth certificate). According to Sue; Aunty

Mary, she was a bit scary... She never married and was cremated 21st October 1980, Grimsby crematorium.

7.1 Janet Elizabeth
(see 5.2)

7.2 Byron John Green
DOB 5th July 1942
Served in Royal Navy.
Lived in Plymouth.
Married Janet Connibear (DOB 21st August 1944)
Had two Children; Jonathon (DOB 14th June 1967) and Austin (DOB 14th November 1969)

7.3 Carol Ann Green
DOB 21st December 1944, died April 2017 of skin cancer.
Married Martin Haxby – Divorced
Had two children; Cenetta (DOB 29th January 1966) and Mark (DOB 31st March 1967, married Lisa)
Married Michael McNally – divorced
Married Mike Lamplugh.

Part Four

The life of Reilly

Letters to the bairns

1998 – 2021

As you can see, this section is a collection of letters written around Christmas time to the bairns, that attempt to chronicle the events of the previous twelve months. They are a sort of potted version of my journals.

I wish that I had started them a lot earlier (both the letters and the journals). But of course it is pointless thinking such thoughts. As the header for each of the later letters stated, 'A wise turtle once said – yesterday is history, tomorrow is a mystery, today is a gift; that is why it is called the present'. The earlier ones had a few of the lyrics from Slade's Merry Christmas song.

The earlier letters contain a lot more detail of whole family experiences. Inevitably though as the years pass and the bairns grow the power of asserting independence rears its head.

The later letters are more of a travelogue of Sue and I enjoying the freedom that comes with being retired grand parents. I'd like to say how bad we feel about the fact that we are so often on holiday of enjoying short breaks while the rest of the family are at work.
I'd like to say that but I can't.

It is amusing now to think that the first one was written on our first home PC. It cost so much that we had to take a loan out to buy it!

So here they are, for what they are worth. They are presented here with the original spelling mistakes and terrible grammar – all mistakes are wholly owned by me!

Dear Lauren, Hannah and James,

I thought it was about time that I started to write down things you might find interesting even if it takes a few years before you read this so I'm dropping you a line to bring you up to date with what was happening in the Reilly household in 1997. As you can see I thought I'd use the new toy to write it (yes it was 1997 when we got our first computer). We bought it to help me while I was studying for a degree, the Masters in Business Administration. The dissertation was handed in just after Christmas but I have to wait until mid March to find out if I've passed or not. The computer is for the whole family to use but your mum's not too keen yet. You all enjoy it of course and have loads of games, some of which are even educational. Not half as entertaining as my Star Trek flight simulator but then you are only young – good things come to those who wait.

Last year saw Hannah join Lauren at school (St. Wilfrid's) and James start playgroup. Hannah also finally mastered her bike and has been improving with practice since then. Lauren is really good on hers and thinks nothing of coming with me on a ten or fifteen mile ride. I seem to have been collecting bikes since getting more into cycling. I started off with my mountain bike, then a racer and then I added a touring bike. The tourer was bought specifically for a ride from Whitehaven to Newcastle which I did with a few mates last spring, 160 miles (and a few pubs) over the course of three days. In return for letting me escape for a weekend your mum got away from it all later in the year for a couple of days walking with a friend in the peak district.

I recently decided (or perhaps your mother did) that it was a bit over the top to own three bikes so I sold the racer to a friend. But then I came across a bargain of a mountain bike so now I'm up to three again. Next year the plan is to cycle to Wales and back and possibly try to raise more money than I did last time (Almost £400 split between the hospital and the school).

As we also celebrated our 10th anniversary last year we decided to splash out on a romantic weekend in Paris. But as this is a family show we can't go into too much detail about that. Suffice it to say I'd recommend it to anyone, you just can't beat sitting outside a French cafe in Paris sipping a coffee and watching the world go by (unless it's sitting outside sipping an ice cold beer).

Summer holidays were in Weymouth and a good time was had by all. Later on we even managed to fit in a trip to Blackpool to see the illuminations. In between this hectic activity I've spent the last year studying hard and writing lots of boring management assignments but hopefully that will pay off. I've been trying to convince your mother to study for a degree but she was put off watching me do mine. We have also reached the taxi driver stage already – swimming lessons for Hannah, swimming club for Lauren, Brownies for Lauren, horse riding for Lauren *and* Hannah. I just can't wait for James to get into something as well.

Lauren won a prize in a Christmas card competition at school and Hannah had her first speaking part in the school nativity play (the year before Lauren had played a cat – not much speaking involved but lots of pawing and purring).

I'm still working at Newark Hospital, and even though I've swapped roles a couple of times since starting with the Trust I've been in the same place for almost seven years now. That's quite a record for me and I must admit that I'm about ready for a change. If it was only that easy of course. Although saying that your mother has been on the same ward for ten years! We both entertain the forlorn hope of retiring from the rat race tomorrow and opening a tea shop or bed and breakfast somewhere in the countryside.

James is a real terror now. He had his third birthday a week ago and got far too much as usual. He's mad about Thomas the Tank Engine and trains in general. He's done nothing but play with his new train track ever since he got it.

This year we're planning to go off to France camping for our summer holidays. That will be much better than some of the other holidays your mum has got planned for me which seem to consist of various jobs including decorating and building wardrobes.

Well I think I've droned on enough now so I'll stop there.
Take care, all our love and best wishes, from,
Mum and Dad
xxxxx

37 Broadfields
December 1998

Dear Lauren, Hannah and James,

Your mother suggested that it was the time again to bring you up to date with what happened in the Reilly household over the past year so here goes.

Let's start with that naughty Lauren Elizabeth Reilly. Can you believe that she actually had to go to the front of assembly to have a reprimand for a fit of the giggles? The shame of it! And what a start to the year.

I on the other hand managed to represent the family slightly better in the world of academia when I achieved my MBA after a profusion of excessive hours of hard labour and mental acrobatics. The antics of the weekend around the graduation are enough to fill a letter on their own, however suffice it to say that it ended in a good party where everyone who managed to retain a memory of the event said that they enjoyed themselves, often having formed lasting (and sometimes intimate) relationships with various bottles and cans. I can personally recommend Morgan's Spiced Rum (and interestingly the spell check brings up the word morgue when it tries to make sense of 'Morgan's').

By the end of spring I was in training for the planned cycle ride (Wales and back) for this year. One part of the programme involved a ride to M's house in Leicester and back on the same day.

For Hannah's birthday (James's was a quiet affair), we all had a trip to Legoland which was actually a very good day out and exceeded our expectation's. I must admit to being slightly miffed at not getting a toy myself but apart from that it was all right.

The cycle trip to Wales happened in late June with me, two mates and another bloke covering 306 miles and several pubs over four days. I managed to raise over three hundred pounds in total which I split between the local school and the hospital I work at.

Summer in France, as far as I can remember, consisted of numerous bottles of wine, lot's of Stella, even more bottles and glasses of the local bierre pression, oh and of course we were there on holiday. Obviously the waves weren't up the standard expected in Australia but we still had great fun with the bodyboard (apart from the occasional wipe-out when we came into excruciatingly close contact with the shingle). You all had great fun with the children's courier and the dad's (not me of course but other ones) wished they could too.

Hannah had a memorable time as she managed to get stung by a wasp and later in the holiday lost one of her teeth. The tooth fairy amazed everyone once again by not only locating us in France but also converting money into francs.

Lauren's birthday treat was a trip to Cadbury's world where the faithful go to worship at the feet of the omnipresent chocolate god. Mum, Grandma and Granddad also succumbed of course but, being vegan, I found it quite easy to resist this pagan ritual.

Being nine also means an extra half hour at night for Lauren before having to go to bed ('not fair' say's Hannah) and the start of – pocket money!

When we weren't busy we were sorting out your social calendar's. Numerous party's and visits to friends houses almost go without saying but there's also Brownie's on Tuesday's (now Thursday), swimming club on Wednesday, Rainbow's on Thursday's, trampoline on Friday's, swimming lesson's on Saturdays... On top of this James is now at Nursery School and with membership of the PSA goes the need to attend the school disco's and quiz night's.

In between times we've been on our usual camping trip's to the peak district and also managed a few days down at Cheddar gorge which was almost rained off but went ahead due to our intrepid nature. That's not strictly true actually. It went ahead mainly as a result of my intrepid nature overcoming your mothers reluctant 'I want to stay here where it's warm and dry' nature. In fact it turned out so nice in the end that we were overcome with the need for retail therapy and bought a couple of bottles of locally produced wine which, although reassuringly expensive were also thankfully very palatable.

Having seen how easy it was for me to slog away and finally achieve my educational goal Sue has lost all avenue's of excuse and plunged into the preamble of attaining a degree herself. Tangible commitment has now been seen in the form of her joining the university library, not to mention the fact that I can no longer call the 'study' my own.

Lauren went on a weekend with the Brownies (the first time away on her own). So we thought we would take the rest of you rabble away as well. Then we remembered that we were looking after the world's favourite canine. Having to pay for it to go into kennels means that a good idea for a cheap weekend was suddenly increased by the cost of a *heated* kennel. Isn't it a good thing that I am so sympathetic to the needs of the hairy little... Still it could be worse.

However, as I can't think of too many things worse I might as well bring this missive to a timely conclusion, so gudday to all of you as G would say down under,

All our best wishes, with all our love from,

Mum and Dad.
Xxxx

Dear Lauren, Hannah, and James,

Well the festivities are upon us once again. So what happened during 1999? Let's start off with James's birthday. As well as a small tea party at home he also had a combined party at Tumble Town with M.

As usual I decided to rearrange the garden as soon as spring arrived and part of the plan incorporated a ton of gravel which your mum decided to move around to the back of the house all on her own!

Valentine's day was romantic with a weekend on our own at K&Y's while you all stayed with your grandma and grandad at Grimsby. Our next weekend away however involved us all in a trip to Buxton to stay in our usual room at the Alpine guest house.

Mum and I also managed another weekend away on our own (again with K&Y) to Harrogate in March where we got in a fair amount of walking and Guinness drinking as well as consuming the entire menu of Wild Ginger, a veggie restaurant in Harrogate itself.

The last day of March also marked the day when James rode the whole length of the garden without stabilisers on his bike.

A weekend in Grimsby at Easter finally let me find out where your mum got her map reading skills. Grandma was sure if we followed *this* path it would lead to the car *eventually*......
Hmmmmm! At least it was a nice warm day to get lost on.

May found us indulging in a small slice of impulse buying. A trailer tent. At about the same time your mum decided to give me a heart attack. I got back home after a day's work to find that not only had she set fire to the vacuum cleaner but she had then sliced through the cable when cutting the grass!

The 'Village Get Together' saw Lauren as a proper belle as attendant to the May Queen and Hannah marching along at the end of the parade. There was a prize for the best stall and as it was a French theme it happened to be a stall where they were all dressed up in stockings and maids outfits that won. Strange that. And for some reason I ended up helping out on the baguette stall with your mum – more pressed than volunteered actually.

Then there's our window cleaner. When we asked him about why he didn't appear to be cleaning the upstairs windows it turned out that he afraid of falling! Perhaps he's in the wrong job.

Our wedding anniversary meal found us at the Salamander again. Lovely meal but it was a bit dis-concerting how many transvestites passed the window during coffee.

June saw us camping at Oakham near Rutland Water and probably the best joke I have ever heard. You girls had been doing 'knock knock' jokes so James decided to try. 'Knock knock' he said, 'Who's there?' we asked, 'James', he said, 'James who?' we asked, 'James Reilly', he said. We laughed all the way to the campsite.

Also by June James had mastered his bike and could ride 16 miles in one go. This was followed in July by his 25 metre badge in swimming. At about the same time Hannah went 'over the rainbow' to Brownie's, and Lauren had her ears pierced (and guess who had to take her).

August saw the anticlimax of the year with the sky being overcast all through the eclipse. They had done such a good job of worrying everyone about going to see the totality in Cornwall that most people didn't bother in the end.

Our main holiday was to France again. As it was toward the end of the season it was just us and three million mosquitoes and a few 'furry creatures' as Hannah liked to call them. It was still enjoyable though and we managed to meet many new bottles of wine during our stay. Amazingly we also managed to become acquainted with some veggie burgers at the local supermarche. When I got home I enrolled for a French course as we intend to go back again.

For lots of reasons the annual cycling trip didn't take place until October this year. Unfortunately I didn't manage to finish the ride this time as my rear block fell off on the way up Winnat's pass. This meant a forced wait in the Castle pub at Castleton drinking Guinness in front of a log fire. As you can imagine I really got upset as I should have been battling back to Buxton through the torrential rain instead.

At the end of October we took advantage of the fact that I had all of the half term off to take a cottage in Northumberland called 'Linkey Law', (part of the Duke's estate as I like to say). The weather was kind and we got lots of walks in as well as visiting Edinburgh on the train. Not only did we manage to locate two vegan establishments but I also managed to acquire a supply of vegan haggis!

Guy Fawkes was remembered in our now usual was of a visit to the Nag's Head in Woodborough and yes, as usual, it rained. So much this time that they had difficulty getting the bonfire lit.

Later in November you girls were both in the Remembrance Day parade, and even more exciting Lauren carried the Brownies flag. While church service went on James and I went back home to tidy up before your mum returned from her weekend walking in the Peak District. The end of November saw us spending a weekend with Grandma and Grandad in the Lake District (just after I had my front tooth repaired and Hannah had her poorly toenail sorted by Sarah the Chiropodist). And it was about this time that we found out how ill your Aunty Liz was (Lauren did a lovely card for me to take when I went down to see her).

James got his 25 metre badge again (my fault of course as I can't retain such facts). Then we bribed Hannah to do 800 metres but grumpy old M only gave her a 600 badge.

This years pantomime was Old Mother Hubbard and we did enjoy it, (oh no we didn't, oh yes we did, boo hiss.....). Lauren did the treasure hunt at the school Christmas fayre with HL, both girls having had their hair sprayed with paint. James had his face painted as a clown, and mum and me won a bottle of wine!

Not much else to report, we are planning to have a new bathroom after I touched the bulge in the kitchen ceiling and a bit fell down (what's that bulge your mother had said). Christmas at the outlaws again this year, then of course it's Millennium mayhem.

Hugs, love, kisses, and best wishes, from,

Mum and Dad.
xxxxx

Dear Lauren, Hannah, and James,

Once again the time has arrived for me to write the festive missive. But first of all I need to tell you about the sad events at the end of last year. Aunty Liz died on the 21st of December 1999. You may not remember her when you read this but we often used to go to her house in the Summer especially when we were camping (you all used to like to use R's pool). Perhaps you remember when M used to (very infrequently) babysit while she and A were in Nottingham. Her death upset me quite a lot and certainly brought my own mortality into sharp relief, especially as I reached the age of forty and she was only 43 when she died. Not the best Christmas present, as I'm sure you can imagine.

In a way I'm also thankful that your Mum and I hadn't arranged anything special for my Fortieth birthday. As well as not feeling too much like celebrating at the time, there was a thing called the 'Millennium Bug', which preoccupied us public servants. It is probably meaningless in retrospect but everyone at the time was convinced that it could be catastrophic! Surprisingly we managed to have a good New Year with you all staying up and lots of people around (S enjoyed setting fire to things).

Later than usual I celebrated my birthday when Mum, me, S&M headed off for a weekend break to Dublin. The flight there was terrible and the landing was worse, not to mention the inability to disembark. First of all the folding walkway wouldn't connect and then they couldn't get the ordinary steps lined up. It took forever to get off!

But it was all worth it and lived up to my every expectation. The bizarre Irish humour of the taxi driver, the city itself, the Guinness tour (of course), the atmosphere, the Carravagio in the National Gallery, the food (amazingly enough), the Guinness itself (naturally), all in all an excellent time and place.

James (or was it me?), got another 'Action Man' for his birthday. He seemed to enjoy his birthday tea, and again had a combined party at the weekend with his friend M. The 'Flying

Superhero' which grandma "just had to buy when I saw it", lasted one day before it was irrevocably broken and made me really happy about the three holes it left in the bedroom ceiling. By February I was also onto my second interview in as many months and beginning to feel like I didn't want any more.

That same month also saw us off to a small cottage near Skipton for the week. It was a real haven in the countryside and helped to recharge all of our batteries. As usual we managed to attract mixed weather – cold *and* wet. One day when we were totally surrounded by mud and sheep and unable to determine a way through the quagmire a farmer on a quad bike stopped and looked at us. "Yer not local are ye?" he said, stating the obvious.

When we did manage to find a warm spell we happened across a herd of bullocks that were obviously not going to move out of our path! However, and this is all the more important to note, given your ages and the winge factor, you all made it up Pen-y-Ghent (through rain, sleet, *and* snow). If you don't think that's an achievement try it now.

On our way back home we stopped off in Harrogate to sample the fare at my favourite Vegan establishment. Garlic bread, potato wedges as a side order, soup with bread to start, and a VLT – trouble was they all came together. Still made room for pudding though.

In March we nipped out for a pint and ended up buying a folding camper near Boston. Perhaps this was because, the day before, Lauren had been allowed down to the library on her own for the first time. I was probably still in a state of concern and dulled senses so that I was convinced that we really needed a camper.

In April we all made it up to Ashington for the weekend and came back in time to take your Mum out for Mother's day at the Ferryboat. In fact April saw a lot of comings and goings. The tooth fairy was late again for Lauren, Hannah started horse riding lessons, James started being bored watching horse riding lessons, Hannah had a weekend camp with Brownies, and Lauren deserted us for a week on her own at Grimsby. In a further exhibit of growing up she even had fish pie!

When we went to retrieve her from the outlaws Mum and I took advantage of the situation and left you all at Grimsby while we escaped to Hull for a meal in Hitchcock's with K&Y. It was very smokey – but I don't think that the majority of it was tobacco.

May was for camping. One night in the garden with you lot, then, after the village get together, the first trip with the folding camper. Mud, mud and more mud.

When M graduated in June Mum and I went to the fashion show. I hadn't realised until then what I'd been missing. I was most annoyed at M's collection. She had fully clothed every model.

Later that month the real Millennium celebration took place at Grimsby (yes I know how unlikely that sounds) but we had everything. A four day heat wave, relatives from America, buying ice in England (it was hot), BBQ's at ten paces as every male resident set about cooking at the same time, a fridge which moved from house to house, the infamous hat game, rounders, races and cross dressing (don't ask). I even got to return to work by train.

To finish the month we all went camping and managed to get Aunty Karen and Uncle Dick-Bob onto bicycles. Richard even managed to have a nice chat with your headmaster Mr A, while I had to make do with Miss B – life's hard.

As June turned into July I deciding to take a job in Barnsley. I arranged to start after our summer holiday and of course part of the decision involved moving us all to the area. One reason for this was the 52 miles each way that I had to travel. We looked at various areas and settled on a new house being built in Penistone.

We had our holiday early for a change but went to France as usual, although this time we went with S, M, E and G. M and I even managed to wangle it so that we took our bikes. It was a good relaxing time apart from the crash on the first day but that's another story. At least I got the opportunity to practice my French. We all mastered body boarding this time and the waves were really great. This was our first attempt at towing abroad as well.

Another effect of the decision to move to Barnsley involved changing the Cinquecento for a Corsa. But with our usual unerring timing we took delivery of it in the middle of the fuel crisis. So our nice new car sat on the drive with an empty tank.

In the autumn Mum and I went off to Hong Kong for a week. It was great. The most memorable thing for me was looking up at skyscrapers at night. We did the usual touristy things; the Star ferry, the tram to the peak, Stanley market, the bird garden, temple street market. We stayed in a posh hotel where it was £38 a head for breakfast, and £7 a pint. Needless to say work was paying not us. It was warm enough to swim on the roof and Mum managed to get sunburnt. But when we got back things were different. It was flood season across most of England. Rivers burst their banks, towns and villages were flooded, and roads were blocked everywhere.

On November 5th prompted by Grandma we had our first bonfire. We burned a fence panel which had blown down in the storms, let off some fireworks, and generally had a good time. When the fire started to die down Grandma sat down and broke the garden table for extra kindling which was very kind of her.

The saga of the house sale went on and on. Our buyers pulled out after signing contracts, but mummy managed to sell the house again twice before I got home from work. All the way through it was a nightmare, not knowing when we would exchange, being homeless for a week. As I write this letter it is still November. We are hoping to exchange contracts on Monday and leave here on the 8th of December ready to move into our new house on the 15th. We don't know where we are having Christmas and the uncertainty is driving me insane!

But, as your Nana always says, "as one door closes another opens!" so we'll just have to see what transpires in the end.

All our love and best wishes, from,

Mum and Dad

xxxxx

Dear Lauren, Hannah, and James,

As Christmas creeps upon us once again here we are ensconced in our new home almost one year on, although we still have the odd bare lightbulb and haven't got round to actually painting anywhere yet. We moved in one week before Christmas last year after a brief period of technical homelessness during which we whiled away our time in a cottage near Ollerton to bridge the unavoidable gap between selling and buying in a very comfortable manner. The large amount of snow that drifted in to greet us on moving transformed the building site into a Christmas card image and turned our steep garden slope into a hillside sled run. There certainly seems to be an excess of weather around here and in fact we didn't see as far as our garage for the first month or so due to the snow, rain, and fog (sometimes all three at once).

I celebrated the relocation, and my birthday, at the Italian restaurant right here in Penistone. It's so nice having somewhere to enjoy a meal and a bottle of wine within relatively easy walking distance. Four days later saw three new pupils arrive at Springvale School. Then, on the following night, there was a total eclipse of the moon that we all looked excitedly out of the lounge window to watch. But, as the light of the moon was obscured we didn't see much, although I suppose that's the whole point of such an event.

For James' birthday this year, with the snow still clinging manfully onto our garden slope (and even falling freshly as we drove along), we took advantage of our new location and popped up the motorway to visit 'Eureka' in Halifax. Later in February, during half term, we ventured up to the Lake District for the first of what seemed like an almost continuous series of holidays. We spent the week in a marvellous cottage called 'High Slakes' near Milburn, which is not far from Penrith. Lots of walking ensued (naturally) with the minimum need for driving and we all had a really good time. In fact it was the first cottage where your mum said she would be more than willing to go back to. It stood on its own along a farm track overlooking a small lake and overlooked by some large hills.

Much earlier than usual our main holiday took place in May and started with us jetting off to America for a week in Florida collecting autographs from Winnie-the-pooh and co., rushing around numerous theme parks, *not* getting splashed by Shamu, getting caught in the odd tropical storm, and generally doing all the exhausting things that go with such adventures. We were so busy for the whole time that we didn't actually manage to enjoy the numerous facilities on the holiday site where we were staying. Thankfully after such a hectic tour we followed on with a relaxing stay at Karen and Richard's where we were introduced to an odd game called 'Bunko' which could only be played after you went to bed.

As promised during their last visit to England R included an American version of camping for us to compare with our own, which could only be summed up as..... interesting, or possibly......different! For example who else would take their own chainsaw to camp – let alone cocktail glasses complete with ice! Or for that matter go camping on an island reached by boat. Then of course it isn't often that the coast guard check to see if you are OK due to the minor storm which swept the lake either. Quite a sequence of events to add to the celebration of your mother's birthday which happened somewhere in the middle of all this.

After the gastronomic desert that had been Florida we were amazed when your Mum and Karen found a well stocked health food shop in Carolina! I think this sudden appearance of suitable ingredients led Karen to amaze herself more than anyone when she demonstrated her considerable abilities as a vegan chef (not forgetting R's own cordon vert abilities of course).

Hannah had the by now obligatory sleep over for her birthday. I returned from a day in Birmingham to find mounds of blood soaked paper on the front lawn, and a trail of red splashes leading up to the front door. One of your friends had ridden straight into James and almost broke his nose. Apparently she didn't know what brakes were for on a bike.

July unfortunately was a final farewell to our old friend T from Nottingham who lost his long-term battle against cancer. We didn't take you to the funeral. It was the last day of term and Lauren's last day before moving on to senior school.

In August, during the genuine school holidays Hannah had her ears pierced but this proved little more of a temporary flirtation with this particular fashion statement. Nature saw to its own foreclosure though as she wouldn't put up with the pain of having ear rings inserted. Perhaps we'll have the replay next year.

The latter part of the summer saw us off on the third holiday of the year would you believe – another week of camping, but this time in Wales. This of course being the year of the foot and mouth outbreak one of the consequences was that our walking (and camping) had been somewhat curtailed. But some of the walks we managed to partake of in the fine wet Welsh weather certainly made up for it. We did manage to fit one more weekend of camping in this year – near Ladybower reservoir with the outlaws – staying on a site at Bamford over August bank holiday while Lauren spent the weekend at nearby Castleton on guide camp.

While Hannah and James returned to Springvale Lauren started at Penistone Grammar in September. At least that should have been the case, but while you girls went back to school on time James had a period of extended holiday, as the new mobile classroom wasn't quite ready.

This years bike ride, later than usual, took me, M and D on a 240 mile trek from Penistone to Hornsea and back along the Trans Pennine Trail. But due to a combination of factors, not least among them the terrible weather in the form of ridiculously strong winds all weekend, it was perhaps the worst ride I've ever been on. At least I managed to raise £225 for charity though.

In September, following a 'G' warning she blew in from Australia with young Harry in tow. Even though she said she was here to visit friends and family, and us, we all knew that she was secretly looking to enrol young Harry at Hogwarts (it was Hagrid who gave it away). Still didn't meet the elusive hubby though.

For Lauren's birthday your mum had planned a trip to the local cinema to see Jurassic Park 3. Unfortunately after you all sat through the opening frames of the wrong film you all left. At least you got to go to a pub for pizza as compensation.

Then in October, on the 11th a terrorist attack on America set everyone to wondering what would happen next – and as I write this its still not too clear even after the apparent defeat of the Taliban.

But life goes on. Hannah is still at Brownies, James still goes to swimming lessons on Wednesday, and Lauren to Guides. We've tried fitting in horse riding, cycling, and walking (lots of walks around Penistone since the paths reopened). We're even tried Ju-Jitsu but that lasted almost less time than it takes to write this letter. Your mum has even started her diploma course.

Mum and three friends also managed to get away for a weekend in October for her annual girls break of walking…….. and drinking………..and food. They stayed in Castleton but this time in a B&B (complete with spiders) so it was slightly further to get to the pub.

Later in October we had the last holiday of the year over half term at Meadow Cottage near Shilbottle. From the windows we could see past Warkworth Castle to the sea and on to Coquet Island. We walked to Alnmouth and back, wandered along the coast from Craster to Dunstanborough Castle, visited Alnwick, and had copious amounts of toast on the fire – courtesy of Nana's toasting fork (a genuine family heirloom). As it was Halloween we also found time to have a carved pumpkin and tell terrifying tales of werewolves and the 'Post of Christmas Past'. When we got back home it was time for the usual pyrotechnics. A bonfire up our hill and a box of fireworks saw Guy Fawkes Night come and go in suitable style.

Last year we missed out on M's birthday shindig up in the Lakes but not this time. Your grandma and grandad came to stay and off went your mum and me for a smashing weekend of walking around Windermere and up Grizedale Pike. Even the meals were great. We spent most of the time laughing and behaving in ways which would have probably got yourselves a telling off but it just illustrates the 'do as I say not as I do' attitude of adults.

Well that just about brings the year to a close. We're getting ready for Christmas now and another New Year in our new home, so it's time to close and wish you all the very best, with all of our love, hugs, and kisses,

Mum and Dad

xxxxx

9 Dalby Croft
December 2002

Dear Lauren, Hannah and James,

Christmas comes but once a year and funnily enough so does this letter (hurrah did I hear?). So what did this branch of the Reilly clan get up to during 2002? Well sit comfortably, grab a drink, warm your toes by the fire and let the past twelve months flow by you once again from one peculiar perspective.

Having celebrated the New Year in style at the outlaws it was straight back to Penistone – leaving you at Grimsby – for Mum to get back to work while I went for a walk up a nearby hill. Surprisingly I happened upon a pub where I set off in search of a hairy dog. A few days later my birthday delivered lots of books, CD's and other goodies as well as a night out for a meal. We were joined by S&M (we were even dragged into the technical revolution by inheriting two mobile phones from them), and J&D. We all trooped over to nearby Dodworth to sample the fare at the Indian restaurant.

By the time you rejoined us James had managed to lose another tooth. Shortly after that Lauren gained a brace. Feeling left out I decided to treat myself to yet another bike.

At the end of January we celebrated Burns night like good pretend Scots with vegetarian haggis for Mum and you, vegan haggis for me and tatties and neeps (OK swede and carrot to be precise) for us all. I even managed to fit in a very poor recital concerning a timorous beastie in an even poorer Scottish accent.

As a pre occasion treat we also fitted in a trip to Magna at Sheffield before we actually celebrated James' birthday at Leicester and enjoyed another of M's world famous curries. With a new seven-year-old gracing the world Mum and I then set off for D&N where we prepared to attend 'the ball'. Dressed up to the nines I went as an inferior version of James Bond complete with a DJ and bow tie while Mum was all glamorous in her new gown.

Continuing the theme started by James I took possession of my new bike on the 7th Feb although instead of getting out on it I spent time in the garden for the next few weekends. But when I finally made it out for a quick 20 miles – it was great, everything I had expected.

Then it was off to Slaidburn in the Trough of Bowland for the week. At least Mum, you and the outlaws spent a week, my stay was shorter and after a few days walking I had to nip back to work, then back to the cottage again at the weekend. All rather hectic, particularly as then you set off for home with Grandma and Grandad while Mum and I went north to Aunty Barbara's 50th complete with a limo ride to see parts of Ashington other tours couldn't reach.

March saw the weather improve and the potatoes went in along with the onions up on the hill. This was just before St Patricks day (which had bizarrely followed our attendance at a pre hysterectomy party but we won't go into that!). We became honorary Irish for the night and had Irish stew, Collcannon and three cans of the black stuff – or at least I did. Perhaps because of the liquid refreshment I think it fair to say that my attempt at an Irish accent surpassed my attempt at Scottish although, like Scottie on Star Trek I probably slipped between the two mid sentence. Twas a grand time so it was, begorah.

Easter weekend brought a visit from S, A and D. We cycled to Dunford Bridge, ate pizzas and had a ride on 'Badger' the steam engine at the Kirklees light railway. D even won the Easter egg draw and you all went on an Easter egg hunt as part of the trip.

When we got home the news announced that the Queen mother had died. They say that she had a good innings but I didn't even know that she played cricket. Probably due to my not keeping track of sporting events.

The weather continued to improve throughout April. This was lucky as Hannah spent the weekend up at Green Moor with Brownies and we started to enjoy more cycling and walking or at least I did – you all just moaned to varying degrees.

We celebrated St. George's day with mince and Yorkshire pudding – so much for British cuisine when you don't eat beef.

By May we had started to camp breaking ourselves in slowly with a gentle one night stay at Hayfield near Manchester. Toward the end of the month we gained another family member in the shape of Cinnamon the Guinea pig, and a day later we became seven (see the connection?) with Flake the rabbit. A week later it was time for Mum and I to celebrate our 15 year anniversary but as it doesn't divide by 7 that was that. The month ended as it started with a 50 mile practice trip in preparation for the real cycle ride planned for later in the year.

In June Lauren went to guide camp near Doncaster and we all went camping at Boroughbridge so that Mum could continue the tradition of celebrating her birthday under canvas. Lauren joined us at the end of the week. As a treat we also went on our fairly regular pilgrimage to Wild Ginger cafe in Harrogate. The day we got back home James had a closer encounter than planned with a local pothole, parted company with his bike, and spent a few days in hospital emerging with his broken arm in plaster.

The annual ride coincided with England playing Brazil in the world cup – some sort of football competition I believe – so our first day found M and I on the road by 6 a.m. When England lost we left the pub where M had watched the second half and pressed on. We spent the next few days covering over 260 miles and cycled through parts of Leicestershire, Lincolnshire, Cambridgeshire, Huntingdonshire and Northamptonshire. Hannah had her birthday celebrations at Leicester while we were away.

The end of June was almost as exciting when my new shed arrived. It's true what they say about simple things.

That brings us to our summer holiday in August – France again, but this time guaranteed sun in the Dordogne. Or so we thought. Monpazier was wonderful but the rain was torrential at times – as it was across most of Europe with many areas having severe floods. But the wine was so good that we brought 50 bottles back – for our own consumption of course.

When the August Bank Holiday arrived we decided to tempt providence by going camping again to Clumber Park – our second trip there this year. But it didn't have to rain (although it did) as almost everyone fell off their bikes in the ford.

In early September Hannah moved up to guides and both she and Lauren both swapped to the new trendy uniforms. Apparently Hannah is a dolphin but if she is I don't see why we are still paying for swimming lessons.   Late in September we had Lauren move up to being a teenager, behaving like one being something that she and Hannah seem to have been practising for years. Her treat of a trip to a pool with waterslides and then the ice rink wasn't such a treat for me as I decided to closely inspect the ice and cracked a rib. Laugh? I did not.

Of course I blamed the earthquake that shook most of the midlands although it didn't officially happen until the middle of the night. But who knows – just because no one talks about pre shocks doesn't mean they don't exist.

Mid October we celebrated K's 40th after dropping the kids off at the outlaws again (aren't we such caring parents?) and spending the night at Hull. We had some drinks which were on fire and it was so cold in the restaurant we didn't know whether to blow them out and drink them or leave them alight to warm our hands.

Toward the end of the month it was off to Bonnie Scotland for a week in a cottage on a riding school. Galloway is a lovely area with lots of good hills to climb and for once the weather was kind to us. As a treat for Halloween we went prepared with a pumpkin. This year's choice was a rather effective carving of a wolf howling at the moon.

No bonfire this year to cheer on Guy Fawkes as Mum was at work and Hannah was rehearsing for Dick Whittington. So we went around to the pub and watched the organised display instead. At least Hannah caught the last half hour.

We had planned to go to the Lakes to celebrate M's birthday like we did last November but he and S couldn't make it this year. So we went on our own (yes you guessed it those outlaws saved the day again). We stayed in a vegetarian country house just outside of Grasmere which had been frequented by Wordsworth, Byron, Burns, etc. etc. Judging by the creaking floorboards they were probably from that time as well. We thoroughly enjoyed our stay –

lovely grub and walks up the nearby crags with views over the mere, although my knee has been protesting ever since. When we got home Mum found out that she had been successful in getting the new job she wanted as a school nurse in Sheffield. She should start in January.

Also in November we saw Lindisfarne in concert right here in Penistone at the Paramount. It was a great night even if the lights did go out during the first song. But it was only to be expected really – we aren't used to so much electricity being used at once up here.

As December arrived this was proved once more at the official turning on of the Christmas lights. The lady Mayor flicked the switch, the tree illuminated, but that was it. A couple of minutes later the next set of lights came on, but the rest stayed in darkness. Not only do we get small amounts of electricity – it also travels very slowly. The whole thing was quite surreal, complete with Sopwith the Camel and Dick Wittington as the warm up act for Santa.

Well that just about brings the year to a close, although we still have a wedding to attend and a surprise 40th to go to. We've been to Meadowhell for the obligatory shopping trip, the beers and wines are multiplying and we're almost ready for Christmas and another New Year in our new home. So it's time to close and wish you all the very best.

Love Mum and Dad
Xxxxx

Dear Lauren, Hannah and James,

Doesn't time fly? It hardly seems any time at all since I sat down to write last years letter. Perhaps I should start this one where that one left off. We ended 2002 with a full blown New Year party for a change – countless children and most of Dalby Croft as well. In keeping with tradition the festive season continued through to my birthday which was celebrated at the very tasty China Court where the head waiter bears an uncanny resemblance to 'Odd Job' from James Bond.

A week later your mum finally got me to paint the hallway and a week after that she had me cladding it. This little piece of DIY seemed to involve a lot of trips to B&Q to buy and return various pieces of timber. But as the wood seemed to enjoy being ferried around I didn't mind too much. It even prompted me to consider taking a plank to work with me for the day but given the number of them there already I thought another one would just cause a crowd.

We missed Burns night for some reason so no haggis this year. Instead I built a summer residence for Cinammon – two rooms and a veranda. What more could a young Guinea Pig wish for. At the end of January your mum left work at the hospital and started as a school nurse in Sheffield.

In February a few things happened. Somehow your mum got me to order a caravan, James had a football party for his birthday at Stocksbridge, and it snowed on your mum's first day at work. Then, after forfeiting many Thursday evenings and the odd weekend for rehearsals Hannah finally played her part in Dick Wittington up at the Paramount. But, with a re-run of a previous year (where I had been poorly and missed the panto) your mum missed the show. The rest of us still had a great time (oh no we didn't, oh yes we.....) watching Hannah smiling dazzlingly throughout the performance.

We were lucky enough to get away at half term again, this time to Gunnerside in Richmonshire (that's posh for North

Yorkshire). The cottage was very basic and worse still the pub had run out of beer because of the snow. Cooking often over taxed the electrics which had obviously been installed by a blind non-electrician. But the walking was great, the pubs all had roaring fires and we had all managed to chill out by the end of the week (apart from the odd occasion where Lauren lost it when sheep ran through a gate toward her). We even managed a dash up to Ashington while we were there.

At the end of February we received the sad news that your uncle, my cousin Gary had died suddenly. Apparently it was a brain haemorrhage. He was 43 years old.

Later in the spring both Hannah and James got into football at school. James even started going to football training. Then the time came to pick up the caravan from the dealer in Huddersfield and of course we had to try it out straight away regardless of the torrential downpour and high winds which lasted the whole weekend. A fortnight later as the world went mad and started to drop bombs we headed for the hills of Derbyshire, just in case, for another outing in the caravan and some walking.

Your granddad's 70th celebration was mixed in with mother's day over a weekend stay at Grimsby. Then it was planning for another trip in the caravan (well we had to get the most out of it having bought the thing), this time up to Boroughbridge.

Easter was spent in the Bohemian atmosphere of S&Ms company and included a ten mile walk for all of us and a 27 mile training ride for M and me. It also meant helping to finish off some of the ongoing home improvements so while M fitted the shower door I engaged in a little arson down at the bottom of the garden getting rid of clippings and other combustible waste.

Your grandma and grandad descended on us for the May bank holiday and we tried to fit as much in as we could – a visit to the Tapas bar in Holmfirth with D&C, walks around Langsett and over the moors, and a meal at Cubley Hall. Also in May Lauren went on residential to the Lake District so we all joined S&M and others with the caravan at Carsington water. But of course the highlight had to be your mum getting a speeding fine. Not surprising really given her defence, 'Well the car was playing up so I had to go fast to stop it from stalling, and anyway I was slowing down when they stopped me.......' Open and shut case really. I should have realised then what was coming in the car department, but more of that later. Then it was Hannah's turn to desert us, going off to guide camp.

Our next break with the caravan was over a long weekend near Birmingham at the pleasant but hitherto unknown area (to us anyway) of Clent Hills. Probably the best bit for me, after the enjoyable walks, was the top notch pint of Pedigree that the nearby pub served. It even managed to provide a vegan meal!

For mums birthday it was her, me and Loz off to T'Iamo's for an Italian while Hannah and James were staying at Grimsby. Mum got a new bike from Decathlon and then we popped out and bought a Land Rover Discovery. The logic apparently was that the old people carrier was on it's last legs and as the caravan is a Bailey Discovery we naturally needed the car to match.

As this years cycle ride approached I increased my training rides and the night before we set off your mum and S went to the dogs in Sheffield while M and I stayed in with a curry and some beers. The next morning it was an early start and up to Ashington for a flying visit to Nana's before cycling down to Newcastle, catching the train to Edinburgh and then cycling down to our first night's stop at a place called Innerleithen. We then spent father's day cycling down to Belford and finished the ride off on Monday back to Ashington in the end covering just over 220 miles.

Later in June Hannah went up to Grammar school for a taster day – the day before her birthday. So how else should we celebrate in what was obviously to become the year of the caravan? You've guessed it – off for a weekend near Rutland water where we were joined by K&J. The weather was warm but nowhere near as hot as the water we got in when we took over two hours to get the chips for supper having made a detour to the pub.

At the end of June the unseasonably warm weather was making the year one of the warmest and driest I can remember. Then we had the run up to our summer holiday. Our neighbours put their house up for sale lured by the ridiculous prices in the housing market, Hannah finished with her swimming lessons, James continued with football, and Lauren continued being a teenager. We were even treated to a flying visit here in Penistone by Nana and auntie Isabel for a weekend. This was followed by N and A who made a literal flying visit over from America and everyone took turns at camping in the garden while I was press ganged into an afternoon of face painting in between raiding the garden for potatoes, onions, beans, gooseberries, and beetroot.

Off to France again in August – this time to a site near to Royan. Bit of a shaky start when I couldn't free the handbrake at 3 in the morning. and I'm sure the neighbours really appreciated my hammering and bashing at that time in the morning, but once we managed to set off we made good time. As usual when travelling through France we took a wrong turn at Nantes which is now almost a permanent feature of the holiday. This year it was hot and sunny and the mosquitoes were out in force. The nearby beach was pleasant but the jellyfish were huge and also out in numbers. One of the highlights of the holiday was the trip to Remy Martin where the cognac wafted smells of Christmas all over us. The beach we found towards the end of the last week, much to Lauren's shock, was au naturiste! We managed to stock up with a good selection of wines for the return trip now unfortunately mostly gone.

James was first back to school in September and then it was Hannah's first day at Grammar school. In the same week mum got her result in the post and had successfully gained her diploma. A week later mum and S went off to London and had a go on the eye while I helped M sort out the garden. Then it was Lauren's birthday. For a change it was a trip in the caravan to Clumber Park – she even enjoyed a Chinese Take away.

I had a day off in October and decided to attempt the Penistone boundary walk. At 16 miles it was good practice for half term which this year we spent in an old spooky cottage called High House at Outhgill near Kirkby Stephen. Open fire, stone flagged floors, and three dead mice – and that was just the start. We went on lots of walks (about 30 miles over the week) with hardly a moan.

We also had the usual pumpkin carving, toast on the fire and ghost stories at Halloween. James unfortunately had his foot burnt when an ember fell out of the fire.

Then it was November and mum took you around to the Britannia to watch the display as I was still travelling back from London. The same week James started cubs and the outlaws came to watch you while mum and I went off for a weekend. First to Edale for the night then a walk up on Kinder before joining M for his 40th.

Later weekends saw mum off to York for a shopping trip (I hadn't realised that was how drinking binge was spelt), and then it was off to Sheffield for graduation day with mum in cap and gown. The same month we saw a tribute band to the 'Bee Gees', mum and the girls went off to Sheffield to see Blue in concert and then mum also saw a tribute band to "Abba".

Now that December is upon us the Advent calendars are out in force, shopping is becoming a full contact sport, and it's psychological warfare as to when the decorations go up.

We went to see James in the school play, sat on those bottom numbing little chairs and watched him walk on his hands. We were met at the entrance by the head who got us to part with money for the raffle, and in the intermission we parted with money for refreshments.

A letter arrived informing us that Hannah had written a poem worthy of publication – we have an author in our midst! Or as Hannah points out, a poet.

Looking forward to Christmas and the whole festive season we will be joined by all the outlaws both from Grimsby and the USA for a small get together. Mum will be preparing a meal for eleven and I'll be preparing to be drunk. So there endeth another year,

Love Mum and Dad

xxxxx

9 Dalby Croft
December 2004

Dear Lauren, Hannah and James,

Would you believe it's that time of year again? It hardly seems a whole year since I last sat down to recount the ongoing saga of life in the Reilly household but let's start at the beginning of the year again and see how we get on.

As usual the year began with my birthday being celebrated in usual fashion with a late night or early morning depending on ones point of view and making close acquaintances with various bottles and cans. Then it was a mad rush of returning to work, school, taking decorations down and putting the festive season back into the loft for another year.

Lots of visitors came and went during January and we even managed to have some haggis, slightly out of kilter with Burn's night but delicious all the same.

For James' birthday we had a trip to the bowling alley after a bit of a chimps tea party. On the way back the car broke down and James thought that the trip back in the tow truck was so cool that next year I'm missing out the party and just ringing the RAC.

Having finally given in and bought a playstation we even managed to get a game that your mum will play – Simpson's road rage.

Mid February was James investment as a cub (lets hope its an investment that pays out sometime). Anyway, your mum can now enjoy sewing badges on again! A couple of days later and it was Valentine's Day so we packed you off to bed and sat down to a romantic dinner for two (very tasty even though I say so myself). Soon afterward I got into training for this years ride and managed the odd 40 miles ride.

Later we spent the weekend with K&J down at Ipswich where we had a grand time and even got to walk along the beach in the bitterly cold wind. When we got back we rolled into Shrove Tuesday and had a highly successful session of pancake making followed by even more successful pancake eating.

It being a leap year your Mum proposed on 29th February – a bit worried when she suggested swapping but then not too relieved to find that she meant the study for the dining room. We moved fast – ready for leek and onion pie on St. David's day, bringing us neatly into March and a weekend in Leicestershire planning the trip to Barcelona.

With St. Patrick's Day approaching I have to say that my innovative Tofu Irish stew in Guinness with herb dumplings was inspired. A drop of the black stuff makes anything palatable in my opinion. Unfortunately not all of you seem to share my opinion.

In an unusual turn of events I ended up doing breakfast in bed for your mum on Mother's Day (spent up at Grimsby this year), while you all watched her opening her presents. Something wrong there but not too sure what. For a treat we went for a Chinese buffet lunch where you all behaved admirably, the food was good, the beer out of date, and the glasses dirty – still, mustn't grumble.

We nipped up to the Paramount when we got back to watch a Queen tribute band called Mercury. It was a good night, couldn't quite understand why the bloke being Freddy kept dancing like Elvis but at least he had no trouble reaching the difficult notes – he just missed them out. After a couple of Guinness at the break they sounded even better.

At Easter we had a long weekend in the caravan at Cannock Chase near Rugeley. It was an excellent base for walking and cycling and for you to moan in turns about both. Hannah and I had a stomach churning night after some dodgy battered chips but we still had fun hunting for Easter eggs before returning home.

At the end of April into May we popped over to Barcelona with to celebrate the collective 40th birthdays. It's a great city, loads to see and loads of veggie places to eat. We got by with minimal Spanish but amazingly had no problem ordering food and drink – even visiting a vegan Buddhist Chinese restaurant!

Mid May and we were off in the caravan again, this time to Blackwall Plantation near Ashbourne. Another nice break with nice company.

Half term arrived and Hannah left for a trip to Holland with school. The next day we set off for Castleton and hit on some glorious weather. But of course the weather turned changeable and consequently we swapped folding money for items we didn't really need but helped to pass the time.

And of course this being Derbyshire it managed to turn glorious again in time for a nice walk to celebrate Mum's big day which we rounded off at the excellent nearby Italian restaurant. Then it was back home to pick up Hannah from school on her return.

Later in June we were talked out of another weekend in the caravan and instead undertook slave labour in the garden at S&M's - a really example of extreme gardening. Personally I blame all those programmes on TV.

Hannah had a pre pre birthday trip to the Paramount to see Harry Potter, a pre birthday sleep over, and a birthday meal at Cubley Hall.

The following weekend M and I set off for our cycle ride stopping for the first night at the suitably dismally named Prospect End B&B in Hebden Bridge. The next day we looped around Leeds and ended up at Boston Spa near Wetherby (another good Italian restaurant here) then cycled back to Penistone on the following day to complete one of the toughest rides we've done even though it was less than 190 miles in total. When we got back I discovered that I'd not taken a key and we had to sit outside until Lauren got back from school to let us in.

At the beginning of July we fitted another weekend in, this time at Rivendale with D&C. It's a good site with walks and cycling nearby and a pub on site – what more do you want?

The following weekend we had what is now almost becoming an annual event – meeting up with K&J at Rutland water. This time it was slightly marred by losing James at one point on the walk but he had the good sense to stay put until we found him.

A couple of weeks later Mum actually made me buy a new bike – how's that for a turn around? So now I've got four again – I'll never understand women.

Now to our other annual event – our trip to France. This year we set off later than usual arriving at Camping de L'Etang on the 20th for two weeks. We had good weather, long cycle rides and a canoe trip on the Loire. Excellent wine and food and it was so late in the season that we had a really quiet time overall. We kept the obligatory tourist excursions to a minimum (Saumur, Angers, Puy du Fou and the Cointreau museum are just some of the places we didn't go to) and maximised our chill out to recharge the batteries.

Lauren celebrated her birthday by babysitting but earlier in September she did get to wander around at the Penistone show and spend money like it was going out of fashion. I also got duped into further extreme gardening this time laying turf all weekend (and that doesn't do justice to the amount of work involved to prepare the ground first!).

To really celebrate Lauren had her friend from Nottingham join us for a weekend at Clumber park where at one point we had eight adults and nine children in convoy on cycles!.

Another weekend joining up with K&J, this time at Penistone, marked the beginning of October followed by half term at Moreton in the Marsh. Not a good idea to caravan this late in the year you might think but it actually turned out to be one of our best holidays so far in a caravan.

Halloween arrived and James went to a spooky do at the Paramount while Lauren and Hannah went out with friends to do some 'trick or treat' mugging of defenceless householders and relieved them of sweets. Your mum and I decanted to the pub which struck us as the most sensible thing to do until it was time to pick up James.

The outlaws arrived to look after you all for bonfire night while me and your mum went off to the Lakes for a weekend of food, drink. company and walking over M's birthday. So now we are into December. The nights are getting darker and it will be Christmas again before we know it – another year past and another to look forward to. Hannah in panto again, James in bother again (eating more than one advent calendar chocolate per day!) and Lauren still struggling with being not quite a grown up (although baby sitting seems to beat minimum wage).

So it only remains for me to wish you all the best of the season and finish off with,

love and best wishes from

Mum and Dad

xxxxx

9 Dalby Croft
December 2005

Dear Lauren, Hannah and James,

A Merry festive missive to you all, Bon Noel and of course a Happy New Year for 2006! But first let's start way back at the birth of 2005. We saw in that New Year at Anstey and managed to stay awake until 2 a.m. having gorged ourselves on a multi course meal extravaganza prepared by Monsieur M. The meal was grand, as was the drink but when we retired to relax on the comfy seats we then had to endure, I mean had the added pleasure of M and A playing their guitars. Thank goodness for the mellow effect of alcohol! Only joking of course – they were both good, or at least I think they were.

My first day back to work after the holidays co-incided with my first day as a 45 year old which is not as comfortable a fit as being 40. I did manage to relive my youth though having received the complete set of Battlestar Galactica on DVD and I finished off reading the Broons. A good Chinese meal at the Cherrydale rounded off my birthday treat. January blew a gale as it continued, and the wind took some of our garage roof tiles with it as it passed. It also managed to aid the rabbit in a brief escape attempt from the hutch and we only spotted this when we saw it talking to a neighbours cat. Hannah started in the panto again and Sue and I celebrated Burns night rather belatedly with a vegan haggis.

February brought James into double figures and he even got to go up on stage when we went to watch the last performance of the panto. The best bit, apart from Hannah of course, had to be when the wicked witch sang a brilliant rendition of Anastacia.

We decided to continue doing things late and celebrated pancake Wednesday instead of Tuesday, and celebrated Chinese New Year a day after it occurred.

We popped up to Ashington in half term and stayed at Isabel's house, managing to fit in a trip to Alnwick and visit Barter Books. When we got back home we managed a short cycle ride, complete with a newly fitted cycle computer on James's bike (we've gone 2.27 miles Dad.......it's 2.36 now Dad..... etc etc)

Toward the end of the month the winter literally found its second wind and deposited about eight inches of snow and closed the Grammar school. James obviously felt left out so, the boy who normally won't eat anything .... decided to swallow a battery. Not funny at the time but following it through with the metal detector was quite amusing.
Fed up with doing things late we had leek, onion and tofu pie the day before St David's day. There's lovely!

By the time St Patricks day got to us we had managed to synchronise with the annual events and had Guinness casserole and dumplings on exactly the right day. Later in March we went to Market Rasen (a great site for cycling and walking) for our first trip of the year in the caravan. Obviously this must have thrown us out again as we ended up having hot cross buns a day late. The Easter egg hunt did happen on the right day but involved a dash up to Grimsby.

When we got into April I started to do a few training rides. But we totally missed St Georges day unless an Indian take away counts nowadays as English traditional food, which it probably does. Mum and S impressed everyone this month by scaling Helvelyn. At the end of the month we went to Newhaven but this was a bit spoiled by the really soggy conditions of the site – although we made the most of it.

Into May and Mum and S impressed once again when they went on a caravan manoeuvring course for the weekend. The rest of the month passed by quietly and we celebrated our anniversary with some fine wines and another Chinese meal this time over at the Flouch. James had a camp over for a friends birthday while the rest of us had an evening in with the Eurovision song contest. At the end of May we nipped over to Grimsby for the weekend and came back to go caravanning at Losehill outside Castleton. And just as we did the year before we celebrated Mum's birthday in the Italian restaurant.

We managed to fit in a trip to K&J and later we saw Hannah turn into a teenager – something she has been practicing for some time now. Celebrations included a trip to Rivendale plus a co-incidental trip to Flamingo Park.

The cycling weekend was around the 24th June this year, setting off from Anstey, over to Leamington Spa (if you ever find yourself there avoid the Trendway Guest House where no expense is spent) on the first afternoon. The next day we wound our way over to Catworth, and then back the next day after that to Anstey. Around 190 miles all told.

James went off to residential at Scarborough and as soon as he got back went off to camp with Cubs. We took advantage of this and had an impromptu camp over at Losehill joining S&M.
We wandered into July and I immediately felt old when Lauren received her NI card and a couple of days later info on pensions! We also had a weekend near Rutland water joined by K&J. In mid July we went over to Barnsley to see James in the school play Hoffman's Medal. He played 'child number two' and had to do it in a Yorkshire accent. Unfortunately we couldn't escape at the end and had to listen to the Headmistress giving one of her interminable speeches thanking everyone and everything (and I'd like to thank the wallpaper, the paint and of course the curtain, lets give the whole place a round of applause shall we).

And then came France! Off we went to Dover, then to Calais, and then Le Mans. The next day we drove the last leg arriving at the site near Le Bugue. The sight of the waterslides on arrival was enough to win over everyone and we settled in for a great break. Plenty of sun, cycling, markets, a bit of sightseeing (Sarlat was magnificent), canoeing on the Dordogne, and generally enjoying doing nothing. Marvellous.

Later in August Hannah declared that she was now a Vegan and of course I got the blame. We fitted in another trip around the bank holiday before we finished with August this time to Elvaston Castle in Derbyshire

1st of September I had a day off and cycled up to the top a hill outside Holmfirth to watch the Tour of Britain cycle by.   Not everyone's idea of fun but I though it was an excellent day.

Lauren reached the age of sixteen without major mishap but talked me into getting broadband. Without going into details this ended up involving us getting a new computer, rearranging the entire house, and all to sort out Laurens iPod. We had a weekend at Clumber Park for her birthday as well and she went bowling with friends to Sheffield

Into October and half term again. Mum couldn't come so I took all three of you to Blackwall Plantation for four nights. We cycled and walked but it was a bit cold by now and wet. In between the raindrops we found a great little place in Wirksworth. The storm on the last night was so bad I thought that the debris from the trees would come through the roof of the caravan.

Toward the end of October we popped over to see S&M going out for a curry as well as eating in. James was a little devil when we got back but I let him off as it was Halloween.

The outlaws joined us for the bonfire up at the showground which was a bit damp because of the wet weather. When we got back I set fire to unsuspecting pieces of wood and had our own fire on the hill joined by neighbours for a drink.

The following weekend I went back to Losehill this time only having James with me leaving all the girls to have a girlie weekend and do their nails and stuff. We had nice days and windy days (even blowing our bikes away at one point) walking and cycling and visiting speedwell.

Around the same time Mum joined university to start studying for her degree. Now the year is drawing to an end and Hannah has started to rehearse for this years panto, Mum has had her shopping trip to York, and we are all starting to prepare for another Christmas here in Penistone.
So it only remains for me to wish you all the best of the season and finish off with,

love and best wishes from

Mum and Dad
xxxxx

9 Dalby Croft
December 2006

Dear Lauren, Hannah and James,

A very Merry Christmas, Bon Noel and Feliz Navidad to you all, and of course a Happy New Year for 2007!

Watching your mum study inspired my decision to take up some studying of my own, as a kind of birthday present, and begin Spanish classes in January. Meanwhile Hannah started rehearsal for the panto once again. The main point of this, it seems to me is to get parents to walk up and down to the Paramount twice a night. However, it also gave us a place to take James on the Saturday after his 11th birthday! He also got to visit 'Laserquest' in Sheffield as well though so don't feel too bad for him.

During February half term we left mum to her studies and trogged up to Ashington for a couple of days, managing to include another visit to Alnwick and the best bookshop in the World, as well as to the Metro Centre on our way back

Valentine's day was nice and romantic – nice meal, nice wine, settled down to watch King Arthur – not romantic admittedly but neither was the part when mum fell asleep during the battle scene.

We managed to hit pancake day bang on the nose but missed Burn's night by weeks. But as the unofficial family motto is 'Nae haggis nae tattie' (which translates to – vegan haggis is better late than never) we made the most of the belated feast.

Late March saw us all in Grimsby and visiting a real French market with real French stallholders and produce and extortionate prices. The crepes were worth waiting for according to the three of you.

Into April and we left mum to study again while this time we all caravanned at Blackwall plantation. Where it promptly rained. In fact we had more of this fine weather all the time we were there apart from the frequent downpours and 35 miles per hour winds – it even managed to throw in some hail for free.

Cinnamon shuffled off its mortal coil if that is what Guinea Pigs do when they cease to be. I came home to lots of tears from Hannah but Lauren was good about it and prepared the shoebox coffin ready for the poor creature to be laid to rest up on our hill. I was asked to pronounce it dead but as it hadn't moved for hours that was a safe enough bet.

Having experienced such fine weather so far this year in April I also made the mistake of mentioning that we might want a new van – the trip to Blackwall had been really cold and the current van didn't have any heating to speak of. No sooner suggested than mum had entered into the spirit of things and a new van was bought without a nanosecond delay. Mum was actually away in the Lakes when we went to pick it up. We got our first use of it at the end of April and headed off to Leek.

Into May and we managed to miss St George's day despite the flags all over the place (and don't even ask me where I put St Patrick's day I seem to have mislaid it entirely this year). What I couldn't understand though was why the flags persisted and even seemed to multiply. Was everyone trying to make fun of me having failed to celebrate our patron saint's day? The answer wasn't revealed until someone told me the World Cup was on this year – how was I supposed to know?

Now the Eurovision song contest – there's an event – didn't miss that one.

Mum and I celebrated our anniversary – 19 years this time – with a bottle of Cava one night and a trip to the Taste of India another. We know how to celebrate.

We spent May half term in the Lakes and this has to be the wettest drought I've known. Admittedly, as I often point out, if it didn't rain a lot up there then there wouldn't be any lakes – it would probably be called the dry hilly district instead. On the day when the sun finally put in an appearance we walked up Great Gable – absolutely excellent view from the top. We finished the week off with mum's birthday before we headed back down to Yorkshire.

Not that I really need one but I bought another bike in June and promptly cycled up and over Holme Moss on it. All part of a cunning plan though as you'll see.

I became worried that the telly was starting to play up as the screen was green most of the time. But it was only the World Cup still on the telly in June!

Hannah had a bit of a three part birthday – a sleep over before, presents and cake on the day, and Flamingoland after. Then as the end of June rushed toward us things were all happening at once – mum finished her degree, we had a trip to T'lamo's as a goodbye treat for Loz, then it was her prom night – limo, ball gown, posh hairdo and some drinks of fizz – then the next day it was up early and off to Manchester airport to see her on her way to America.

July brought proper sport to the telly at last – Le Tour de France est arrivee. When we next took the van out we even found time to frequent a little French style bistro in Wirksworth – strange without Loz though.

James also finished his stint at Springvale and we took the opportunity for a weekend over at Castleton in the van as a last weekend away before our main holiday.

The end of July saw us off to France again but it was still strange without Loz – even stranger that the customs asked which of our two remaining children we were leaving over there as the caravan club had booked four of us on the crossing over to France but only three coming back. S&M joined us as did the Hills on this occasion.

We actually returned to the same site as last year which was a bit of a first for us. It did make things easier though seeing as we already knew our way around the locale. The highlight was probably my attempt at almost drowning us all in the river when the canoe capsized but hey what are holidays for if not adventure. E gets the medal of honour for rescuing me when I cut my foot so bad that I couldn't get out of the river.

The day after we got home I popped in to hospital for an op on my nose and then had a couple of weeks off to recuperate. Obviously as I'm writing this it must have gone OK.

At the end of August we managed another outing to Grin Low. Did I say that the best bookshop in the worlds was in Alnwick? I might have to reconsider that assertion after finding perhaps a better one on numerous floors in Buxton. All in all I only had two days in work in the whole of August – that's the sort of month I could get used to!

Yet more excitement came along to top it all off when the Tour of Britain cycled through Penistone! I managed to talk your mum into taking you down to watch them go past while I cycled over the Strines to watch them do the hillier section on their way to Sheffield.

So now into September – me back to work properly, James joining Hannah at Grammar school, and a newly returned Loz off to college in Huddersfield. Even managed to get your mum onto a proper bike, complete with drop handlebars.

We won't mention the fact that Loz displayed sheep like tendencies and spent the first few days on the entirely wrong course – at least she had wondered why there was no mention of childcare whatsoever!

Having missed out on a cycling weekend Mum and I left you in the hands of the outlaws and headed off to scale Snowdon. We stopped in the best veggie B&B ever and the day we climbed was one of the hottest this year. We made it to the top, and on the way back even paddled in the stream to cool off our overheating feet.

Then it was Loz's turn for a birthday – 17 years old. A creature of habit like us she celebrated in the van at Clumber Park with her friend from Calverton.

October saw some of my cunning plan come to fruition when your mum got her own proper bike!

October half term saw us in Spain having flown from Manchester – it was foreign enough to be nice but too English at the same time. We managed all right with the language and even the local transport, until the day we came back. We had two taxis James and I headed for the train station – girls and mum argued too long over who would speak to the other driver and turned right as we turned left!

S&M joined us around his birthday and bonfire night. But instead of attending the usual display we went to an Irish night at the White Heart so I suppose I found St Patrick eventually if he lives at the bottom of a Guinness glass.

The band from Dublin got better as the drink flowed – but that could just as easily have been an illusion brought on by the drink. I still indulged my pyro tendencies on the 5th itself burning all manner of things up on the hill then playing soldiers with James in the bushes for a while until mum called us in.

November ended with a trip to Sheffield for me and the outlaws to watch your mum graduate. As usual it was quite a ceremony and I always like to see such a collection of intelligence in one room all wearing silly outfits – particularly the Doctors in their floppy pudding hats. It was all very grand and we were all very proud of her.

But now its December and you are already demolishing the Advent calendars to start the real run up to Christmas. I'm sure we'll have a good one, so lets end as the letter began with fondest wishes to you all and the best of the season,

love and best wishes from

Mum and Dad

xxxxx

9 Dalby Croft,
December 2007

Dear Loz, Hannah and James,

Merry Christmas and a Happy New Year for 2008!

How things change! Last New Year Loz spent the first New Year away from us – over at her friend's in Huddersfield. So it was only four of us up until 2.30 seeing in the New Year. And would you believe it – Steve McQueen didn't get over that second barbed wire fence again. Perhaps he will next year, although I reckon he could do with a different motorbike.

Mum and I went out for my birthday for a change and had a meal at the White Heart. They did a good effort at catering for a vegan but it was far too overpriced. I had a side order of chips and when it came there were only six, very nicely arranged of course.

January was wet and we didn't know at the time but it was a good indication of the weather for a lot of the year to come. We even fell ill and succumbed to flu apart from James. Thankfully we recovered sufficiently to celebrate Burns night with haggis, garlic tatties and neeps.

Grandma's 70th birthday bash followed closely on so we popped over to Grimsby for varied celebrations. The highlight had to be the overheard discussions of the various guests debating what songs they wanted playing at their funerals!

When it came around to James' birthday he couldn't see why he couldn't have the day off like I'd had for mine. So, to make up for him having to attend school, we went out to Cubley Hall that evening for a meal. The next night we extended the celebrations by going to the panto, oh yes we did. And to finish off a weekend long birthday we took him and a few mates over to Sheffield so that they could indulge in 'Laser quest'.

February brought a decent amount of snow and unfortunately meant cancelling our first planned weekend away in the caravan. But it wasn't deep enough to stop Hannah going skiing to Italy the following week. We took her to the bus at 430 in the morning and thought how ironic it would be if we had more snow here than Italy.

Hannah really enjoyed the trip and came back full of enthusiasm for this new activity with vast potential to spend money on. Now she wants to learn Italian and ski forever.

We managed to have leeks on St David's again and this year. I decided to practice for our next Pagan ritual of celebrating St Patrick's so the odd pre event Guinness tasting session went well. The Irish stew and colcannon was grand on the night.

About the same time we celebrated Mother's day with a pizza and set about getting planning permission for the extension which we rather grandly called the 'sun lounge'. Work wouldn't start until May at the earliest but given the snow, hail sleet and temperatures of −6 at night we reckoned we could wait. Toward the end of March Hannah went on another trip with school − Belgium this time.

We finally got a trip in the caravan as April fool's day approached. No Loz (home alone) or Hannah (sleep over at friend's) just James this time, and G who was joining us for a week.

Easter was hectic − a quick dash up to Ashington then a dash down to Leicester. The weather was great, unseasonably good and didn't give a hint about the rubbish weather summer had planned for us.

By mid April I had Mum into training for our ride in June. She made it up Holme Moss, which is no mean feat. The next day I ran the 10K run in Sheffield. I'd hoped to beat the hour and made it in just under the 59 minutes as well as actually running the full distance so I was pleased with that. I can also say 'done that, got the tee shirt' as they gave free ones away at the end.

We managed another weekend in the van before Mum and S went off to the Lakes for their annual girly walking weekend. I headed in the opposite direction for the weekend and dropped Loz at Calverton on the way to Leicester.

We had a nice time at May bank holiday at a small site outside of Ashbourne and a fortnight later we were in Grimsby again. This time it was the world famous plant sale in aid of …… well, let me just put it this way, I'm happy to support a good cause but I'm not sure about raising money so that your mother in law can run at you with a defibrillator. If you hadn't already had a heart attack you would pretty soon!

Then came our land mark wedding anniversary – 20 years! To prove that romance isn't dead I got some walking boots and Mum got some cycling clothes. To celebrate in style we got ourselves suitably overdressed and went for a vegan meal at a typically hippy place in Sheffield. And to top it off Mum got to spend quality time with Hannah in the van at Buxton while I went to work, Loz went to Devon with her friend and James went to Holland. The weather was great though and we had a glorious day for Mum's birthday the next weekend.

One week before our planned ride I managed to get Mum out on the bike again but this was when the weather began to change. A week later the whole area had more water than it knew what to do with. Sheffield was closed off and the roads all looked more like rivers.

Then came the planned cycling weekend for Mum and me, and the rain continued. But we still set off toward Bawtry, occasionally being turned back from our route by police and even seeing cars up to their windows in water. But we got there and arrived to sunshine and a warm afternoon. The rest of the ride was just as changeable with the roads closed at inconvenient places and the weather changing between wet and dry without warning, but we got back home safe and sound after 160 miles and no real mishaps.

Hannah celebrated her birthday by being just taller than Mum but was disappointed at not being able to use the garden for a sleep over due to the work continuing on the sun lounge. And still the rain came down, so yet again we ended up cancelling a planned weekend away as it probably wasn't a good idea to camp near a reservoir in the circumstances especially as the second word in Rutland Water is …. well, water.

But then it was almost summer and we loaded up the caravan and headed off to top up my annual allowance of France. This year both Mum and I had proper bikes so the cycling was even more enjoyable than usual. The down side was that if we had returned to the site we had been to for the last two years I could have seen the Tour de France go past.

We left the site, the lake, the beach, the wine, the bread and the lovely weather of France behind and came back to the ongoing puzzle of where was the summer in England. Aunty Isabel celebrated her 60th and we finally got the sun lounge finished.

We did spot a bit of fine weather when we went off for the weekend to Buxton. The highlight was the wires high up through the trees at 'Go Ape', complete with scary zip slides and Tarzan jumps. When we got back home we picked up our new car.

The following week it was my turn for a weekend away a bit shorter than usual with a two day ride from Leicester. A long 105 miles on Saturday followed by a short run of 35 miles on Sunday. Soon after that I took the day off and cycled over to watch the Tour of Britain as it flashed by.

September came and went with a weekend of Duke of Edinburgh for Hannah and lots of gardening and cycling for me. I even managed a few rides in to work and back. Oh and there was a small celebration as Loz made it to 18! The party went on until 1, she had lots of friends around and received loads of pressies, and the next day I thought I needed something as well so off I went with M and bought another bike.

Early in October Mum, James and I went for a little cycle ride around Barnsley that ended up being 28 miles off road and quite challenging. October also found us at K&J's sailing along the river Orwell. A great time was had by all and it was so relaxing.

We were away in the caravan for October half term but once again without Loz who had a whole week on her own at home and had to contend with the 'trick or treaters' without us. We went to a site near Bolton Abbey and had lots of walks and an obligatory trip to the vegan bistro at Harrogate.

November seemed to go by really quickly. No sooner had I indulged in a bit of pyromania to celebrate bonfire night than almost the whole month seemed to have flown by. Children in need came and went and the weather has turned from autumn into winter as the temperatures dropped. Now it's December and the next stop is Christmas! We've already had one Christmas dinner and some folk already have their tree and lights up.

The outlaws are coming to us this year and then we'll be off to see in another year with S&M before it all starts again with some resolutions to make and then break.

love and best wishes for another year,

from

Mum and Dad

xxxxx

9 Dalby Croft
December 2008

Dear Loz, Hannah and James,

Merry Christmas, Bon Noel, Feliz Navidad, Happy New Year, Bonne Année and Feliz Año Nuevo for 2009!

We celebrated the end of 2007 with a trip to Cropston where long dresses and black ties were the order of the night. Then a few days later it was a quiet night in for my birthday. Almost by tradition we missed Burn's night by one day but it didn't stop me forcing you to eat vegan haggis again.

We celebrated James birthday and progression to the teenage years with a trip to Sheffield for ice skating for him and his mates. Loz continued with college Han prepared for exams or her prom night (not sure on the split of effort there) and I prepared to study French by developing a taste for Cognac. We did manage to hit Shrove Tuesday though and demolish a pile of pancakes.

Mum and I celebrated Valentine's Day with a romantic 16 mile walk in drizzle and mist as part of her training for the Moon Walk. At the end of February the Earth literally moved when we had an earthquake!

In March Mum and I did manage to fit in a short weekend at a hotel – it was nice but as usual they were surprised to find that I was still vegan the next morning and didn't want the black pudding.

We'd had a little snow early in the year and it returned with Easter so our egg hunt (probably the last one of those as well now that you are all growing up so fast) was indoors rather than the garden. Basically it wouldn't be cool to be seen running around outside and anyway (apparently) there is no Easter Bunny. Well that's news to me!

We managed a weekend at Clumber Park in April but Loz stayed home. Our next trip for May bank holiday co-incided with Mum going off to Crete so us four spent two nights in Derbyshire at a site that we won't be revisiting unless we all convert to being 'Chav's'.

Mum set off for the Moon Walk in London on the 18th May. She completed it in 7 hours and 55 minutes which was excellent.

162

For our anniversary we went over to Rivendale and spent the weekend on our bikes on the nearby trails. A week later we had a visit from K&J for the weekend. Then it was Mum's birthday on the Monday so we all went off to Cubley Hall for a meal.

Hannah's 16th arrived later in June and so did a load of girls, high pitched squealing and presents. A week later we dropped her off at Manchester airport and then off she flew to visit with Aunty Karen in America for a couple of months.

In July Mum and I set off for a weekend bike ride starting off with a ride over to Beverley, then on to Wetherby the next day, and back home again the next. Just over 190 miles covered in total – then it was off to see the doctor with a bad knee. Later in July we had to take Loz in to hospital for an overnight stay to sort out a small abscess – we're getting our money's worth out of the health service at the minute.

Into august and it was our first main holiday to Spain – no France this year. A couple of weeks on a site near Santander where we thought that we'd lost James and were helped by a nice Spanish family to call the police. Not sure that Mum enjoyed the crossing back through the Bay of Biscay though as it was rather rough.

We had a four night break with S&M (no Loz again) at Rutland water at August bank holiday to round off the month and then on the 2nd September Hannah returned and noise levels resumed normality. We also fitted in a flying visit to Ashington, and then later to Hull (Y's 50th) where the long dress and black tie put in another appearance. Then it was Loz's 19th and she opted for a trip to Pizza Hut. A week later I had my end of course assessment for my French certificate level but the results take ages.

The first weekend in October found us at K&J's house for another trip on the river, and a week later I tested my knee with a 100K (sounds more impressive than 63 miles) ride up and down the hills in the Peak district.

For October half term we went on a trip to Belgium which was great, and on the way back nearly died which was not great. We (actually me – because I was driving) spun 180 degrees with the caravan still attached on the M1 and ended up facing the wrong way into the traffic. The police kindly closed the motorway to let me face the right way and we set off again.

We remembered the 5th of November but no fire for me this year as you were all over at various events with your friends. Also in November, as seems to be the case each year, Christmas started far too early with shops dressing their windows and towns switching on their festive lights well before December was even close.

But at last the weather turned colder and we even had the occasional drop of snow to let us know that winter had really arrived and we were into December, counting the sleeps until Christmas, buying presents, and merrily wrapping them up.

So, as we begin the countdown to another Christmas it's time to draw this letter to a close and wish you a very Merry Christmas with, love and best wishes for another year,

from

Mum and Dad

xxxxx

Dear Loz, Hannah and James,

Merry Christmas, Bon Noel, y Feliz Navidad por 2009, Happy New Year, and Feliz Año Nuevo et Nouvelle Année heureuse pour 2010! Last New Year was really quiet celebration, perhaps a reflection of how grown up everyone was – Loz and Han both out for the night and James stayed in his room – no bubbly for us grownups and then straight off to bed – bah humbug! But a few days later and things improved with the arrival of my birthday and I became the proud owner of an iPod touch before celebrating with a meal at the Indian. That's the trouble with having a birthday in the middle of winter – the waiters always outnumber the customers. And as for the rest of January it was easily summed up - dark and cold. James kept on with his karate, Han continued to excel at spending, and Loz fitted driving lessons around a trip from college to Disneyland Paris.

My French course started again in February and shortly after that we were off to Zaragoza (without Loz) to visit our familia español for a few days. We had a great time, taxed my linguistic abilities (at least Hannah gave it a go as well), and discovered that what the Spanish call 'churros' is the same as the French call 'chi-chi's', but it translates from Spanish into a rude word in English (not helped by our explanation that they are really nice dipped in chocolate)! James managed to top off the experience by leaving his phone in the toilets at Stansted on the way back. But even more amusing, when we got home we found out that we hadn't even paid the bill for the hotel.

Loz had her orthodontic operation in March she had been waiting so long for, which went well. To celebrate I had some Guinness as it was also St. Patrick's day.

For Easter we went with the van to Rippon and let the bairns (again no Loz) have a day at Lightwater Valley while we went to the Brewery at Masham (Theakston's this time). As April drew to a close I couldn't bring myself to celebrate St. Georges Day – mainly due to the news that Graham Norton was taking over from Sir Terry for the Eurovision – what is the world coming to?

In April we also caught up with some other friends that we met in Spain – M and M and then in May we went to a campsite outside of York that Hannah hated but we thought was great. We even managed a trip to visit a Buddhist retreat as well as finding something vegan to eat at El Piano. The next weekend mum went off to Wales with her girly gang for a walk and a stay in an hotel. M came up to us and we did much the same thing – beer, pub, takeaway and wine, films, and more beer. Toward the end of the month we met up with S&M for a long weekend at Tewksbury – good cycling country but apparently prone to flooding – even the toilet block was up on stilts!

Mum had been so impressed with the hotel in Wales that she had booked us in for a night in June as an extension of her birthday weekend. We went for two nights and spent the second in the vegan B&B that we have visited before. Unfortunately the weather was atrocious so we only managed one walk and frankly we shouldn't have attempted even that in the conditions. Also unfortunately the food at the hotel didn't live up to expectations but it certainly did at the B&B as usual.

By mid June it was time for our bike ride and Mum and I set off in sunshine for a change. Defeated for only the third time ever by a hill we got to Buxton the first night and two days later with 110 miles covered (mainly vertical with all the hills around here) we got back safe and sound. Then it was a combined celebration of father's day and a birthday weekend for Hannah with us all going to Cubley to celebrate.

July arrived and with it the week's residential at Caen University. This probably brought on my understanding of French faster than any other aspect of my course so far. After that we had a further two weeks in France for our holiday, first of all near the Normandy beaches and then further down the coast.

Almost as soon as we got back it was a quick switch of languages as August ended, and we welcomed our friends over from Zaragoza so that I (helped by Hannah) could do terrible things to the Spanish language once again. The month ended with a bank holiday break with the van near Belper, again with S&M.

September brought the second ride of the year – this time M and I up to York and back. We stayed over of course and had to sample some of the beers just to be polite. Another 120 miles chalked up.

The following week we dashed over to Grimsby, celebrated the 50th wedding anniversary of the outlaws, and then dashed back again. Then it was Lauren's birthday and a meal at a Chinese restaurant before I spent three days down in London for a course with work. She then went off to London with Ricky for a weekend and didn't enjoy the London eye one bit.

When it came to half term in October we had both boyfriends with us and so needed two cars as we set off to Scotland for a week in a cottage in Ayrshire. Despite the weather and the fact that I missed two days being uncharacteristically ill we still had a good time including carving three pumpkins.

I managed to set fire to some wood in the garden to mark yet another soggy 5th of November and began to think about my impending half century – so I rashly ordered some Port from the 1960 vintage to have a bottle of something special to mark the occasion (there'll be Champagne as well of course). At the end of November we even fitted in a practice Christmas with the outlaws (evidenced by the photo below) as they will be America for the real one. We did however draw the line at eating the Christmas pudding that they had cooked last year.

So, as we enter the last few weeks leading up to another Christmas it's time to bring this letter to an end and wish you all a very Merry Christmas and a Happy New Year,

with love and best wishes for another year,

from

Mum and Dad

xxxxx

Dear bairns,

Merry Christmas!

What a great year for weird dates –01.02.2010, 08.09.10, 10.10.10, 01.11.10, 12.11.10 etc. – quite a binary year all in all; I bet computer geeks loved it.

It was my 50th birthday year and I had a 50 year old bottle of Port to celebrate it with. Mum and I went off to a nice hotel in the snow for my birthday weekend which was great and we got back to a house that was decked out with banners and balloons and a nice homemade birthday cake (obviously the house wasn't decked out with the cake but you know what I mean.....)

In traditional manner we marked Burn's night with a haggis, tatties and neeps – and actually had neeps this time – with which we were quite underwhelmed. A short while later our loveable 14 year old lump turned into a 15 year old lump on his birthday in February. James is consistent though and continues to split his time between the playstation, his girlfriend, and karate (and I'm probably right with that order).

With the girls now all grown up it was only Mum, James and I at half term – spending the week in a tiny cottage in February near Ashbourne. It had a proper fire for toast and was just right and so cosy even in the snow. Ashbourne itself was boarded up for the annual 'up'ards versus down'ards' football match. We had a nice Valentines meal and pancakes for shrove Tuesday before heading back home and then returning to work.

A week apart in March both girls passed their driving tests – another sign of age if you ask me! For Easter we went off in the caravan, (again without the girls) and stayed near Helmsley. Plenty of walking and cycling, loads of nice country pubs and overall a relaxing time had by all.

In April, as Iceland hadn't been in the news for some time, it decided to have a volcanic eruption and close most of the airspace over Europe. In response to this environmental disaster we had another couple of weekends away............ until we had to save our money. Hannah managed to damage both of our cars at once. She backed Mum's off the drive straight into the side of mine and locked them both firmly together – I thought it was hilarious.

But pretty soon it was back into the caravan took advantage of the unseasonably warm weather in May which lasted until our anniversary before turning into wet windy and cold again ready for the bank holiday weekend. We celebrated Mum's birthday on our return from a particularly wet weekend in the van with a trip to see the new Robin Hood film at the Paramount.

We celebrated Hannah's 18th at a Chinese restaurant and the late June warmth let us continue the celebrations, including having a barbecue, before Hannah took E 'round 'tarn' to help complete her education.

Summer came at last and in August we went off to France where we had a great time with P and E including a visit to Paris before going on to the campsite near Troyes in the heart of Champagne country. While the weather was mixed we managed to enjoy ourselves on our bikes along the miles of cycle tracks that wound around the side of the lakes (while Hannah stayed in the van most of the time). We blew a tyre on the caravan on the way home and the weather all the way back was ferocious. So when this is taken with our previous adventure in off road caravanning no-one is really keen to go on long journeys towing ever again!

Sadly Mam passed away this year at the age of 89 – on her birthday. We all went up to the funeral and in a strange way as is often the case it was also good to see everyone even though the occasion itself was incredibly sad.

On a happier note Loz completed the Glasgow 10K a week later in a time of 1hr 17mins 6 seconds. The same weekend M and I rode to York and back on our bikes and Mum and S shopped.

A week later Loz had an unexpected stay in hospital with a hernia! Then it was her 21st and we celebrated with a Mexican meal at Chiquitos. She continued to celebrate for the rest of the week culminating in a trip into Sheffield for the night.

In October we three musketeers went off to Zaragosa for half term where I mangled the Spanish language again and Mum lost her phone. We had a great time and visited some lovely little pueblos up in the mountains.

This year, much to the surprise of the bairns, we celebrated Nov 5th with some fireworks. Although it must be said that the initial surprise and joy didn't prevent a note of sarcasm creeping into the 'whoooo's' when the less spectacular ones went off – but let's face it they were only 'two boxes for £10' from ASDA so what could one expect.

November 1st was officially the start of my Spanish course even though I've yet to receive my results for French – the snow returned as November turned into a cold December and at the same time Loz received her first pay packet.

Hannah reckoned to get 20% of a bike at Halfords and until then Mum had decided that we would celebrate my next birthday on July 4th (due to an inability to figure out any more presents so close to Christmas).

So, with less than four weeks to go before another Christmas comes out to play it's time to round off this letter and wish everyone a very Merry Christmas and a Happy New Year in 2011,

with love and best wishes for another year,

Mum and Dad

xxxxx

Dear bairns,

Merry Christmas once again!

After another quiet New Year last year, celebrated at S&M's (without any of our children this time I might add) I strolled through yet another birthday accompanied in grand style by a bottle of Drappier Champagne – now promoted to being the official Champagne of the Reilly family.

Toward the end of January we visited the outlaws over at Grimsby and found out during the after dinner conversation that on at least one occasion Mum's dad managed to get very drunk on Schnapps (with the rather random result that they ended up at the guest house that Bernie Winter's mum ran….I suppose you had to be there…..). And of course as January drew to a close it was haggis tatties n' neeps for Burn's night.

So then we said hello to February. On the 1st of February I had a meeting at work where I was informed that I was to be made compulsorily redundant but the 2nd was a more cheerful day as we had James' birthday to celebrate, for which he requested that I made quesadillas. Then it was Chinese New Year so we had a take away of course, and we finished off these elongated celebrations with a trip to the 10 pin bowling in Sheffield followed by more food than anyone could possibly need to eat.

A week or so later Mum and I went off to Sheffield on our own to see a play (Blood Brothers – excellent!), have a meal and stay over for the night; taking full advantage of the inclusive access to the pool and spa. So, as I sat in a room full of steam contemplating another month going by, I began to wonder what to do when I stopped earning a wage…' I know', I thought, 'why not buy another expensive bike that I don't really need!' I did feel a tiny bit guilty about that until Mum helpfully suggested a purchase herself. 'Why not buy a caravan as well?' So we did!

Soon it was St David's but instead of leeks for we opted for curry – perhaps a new economy drive was at the back of our minds. But by

Pancake Day we were back on track and I made a load of them to satisfy the whole family. Then, horror of horrors – I missed out on St Patrick due to a sore throat! Was this some kind of punishment for buying a bike? I hoped not or I might end up seriously ill when the caravan eventually arrived.

We picked up our new caravan in early April (and I was not struck down by the anticipated plague or other punishment) so we set off immediately into the wilds of Derbyshire to try it out. Then I got a firm finish date from work – it would be near to the end of May. Easter was unseasonably warm and we went in for a bit of BBQ action to celebrate. We hid the eggs around the house – and probably as an escape from this Loz and Ricky went off and bought a house in Grimethorpe.

April finished with a trip to Rutland water which coincided with a televised wedding. Some famous people were getting married – and apparently one of them was the sister of the bridesmaid. Now this bridesmaid was wearing a rather tight dress and had a really nice … Initially we blokes weren't at all interested at all and it was only the women who were in the van watching TV, but when the bridesmaid showed up it was a different story!

James started his exams in May and both of you girls started new jobs. Hannah's started on the 20th and that was the day I finished work. Then I read somewhere that apparently the world was planned to end the next day – 'typical', I thought, 'I won't even get a lie in to celebrate my new found freedom from the rat race'. Of course it is always best to take these sensationalist announcements with a pinch of salt and possibly more likely was the other story that caught my eye that day; the US government publication of 'What to do in the event of a zombie outbreak'.

I woke on the 22nd May and apparently the world hadn't ended, so it was a good job I'd sorted out a present for our wedding anniversary… more good food and champagne!

And of course in June it was yet more champagne for Mum's birthday, to celebrate and commiserate; that she still had a job while I was enjoying the life of Reilly. We celebrated further by having another night out in Sheffield and watched Hobson's Choice.

We briefly caught up with Loz and Ricky who were there as well but they went to see the Jungle Book.

By mid June I (or more accurately Mum) had decided that I should become a self employed management consultant – and as soon as I did the internet connection went down. So I spent the next few days having long conversations with a nice chap in India having negotiated the various options (if you want to give up the will to live please press 1 now followed by the hash key otherwise hold for one of our operatives who will answer you as slowly as possible). I managed to get by with a combination of visits to cafes with wi-fi and the odd trip to the library until I finally got confirmation that an engineer would come out (would you believe it was an email confirmation of course!). In the end I had to upgrade to a new router and this coincided with James 'up-grading' to blue belt at karate.

At the end of June I put my suit back on to act as chauffeur for James and Lydia to the prom and then a couple of days later I was off to Manchester to drop him at the airport for his trip over to America. I was by this point considering joining the women's institute – having made my first few jars of jam... (Why do gooseberries make purple jam?).

To top off a busy June Mum, Loz, and Hannah all ran the Race for Life in Sheffield (32, 43 and 37 minutes!) Then it was time to switch to bikes a week later and Mum and I went off to Wetherby for the weekend.

As the summer holiday approached Hannah decided to have a short stay in hospital immediately before the rest of us set off for France and the outlaws kindly came down to look after her as she recuperated from taking her own discharge against medical advice. So then it was August in France again for a pleasant break from reality. Afterward I was back in England for only one day before I started working again – only a day and a half a week though so not too much of a shock for the system to cope with. And as I had to pick up James from Manchester that Thursday I only did one day of work in total that first week.

A couple of weeks later Mum and I returned to France without you bairns and had a great road trip with a stay at Chateau de Pizay, champagne (Drappier of course), burgundy wines and even some mustard in Dijon.

Continuing to dispense money recklessly I wandered into town in September and paid the mortgage off – then surprised Mum with the news, so more Champagne Drappier was consumed! What a marvellous feeling to be mortgage free.

A week later it was off into gale force winds for another weekend cycle trip, this time with S&M to Oundle and back from their house. We found a really nice hotel to stay at and Oundle is a pleasant little village to wander about.

Then it was just all too much! 16 September saw Loz and Ricky moved into their new house, Hannah moved into her Uni digs that same weekend, James didn't move at all (until he realised that he was going to be the only one in the house to be told to do jobs – then he made himself scarcer than usual), and Mum started a list of jobs....

October came in with another mini heat wave – we were sunbathing during our caravan weekend in Derbyshire. Later we spent half term in the Lakes with James. Mum had a call from Loz to say that she had just been proposed to in front of the orang-utan enclosure at Chester Zoo.

Luckily it was Ricky who had proposed so the house purchase wasn't going to be a problem....

Halloween came out as soon as it got dark but with more 'trick or treaters' this year. I spent the evening giving them things to make their teeth fall out while everyone else pretended they were on the phone or couldn't hear the knock on the door.   We even had a couple arrive a day early in fact – in the guise of my two sisters who came down to visit for the day!

No bonfire this year though – James was on residential, Mum and I were at M's for his birthday celebration. Then it was the middle of November, the dark nights were drawing in, so we wondered what to do next – 'I know', said Mum, 'let's spend even more money'. So we had some builders come to dig tons of earth out the garden to create a walled courtyard and some retaining walls to create more useable space behind the garage. Great timing of course as it was Loz's engagement party (far too much food as I knew there would be) in the middle of all this chaos and mud – and we had 15 people stay over at our house for the night.

At the end of November Mum went off for the weekend with her girlie walking cronies leaving me and James to Bond... James Bond... And now that we have passed the tipping point it is downhill toward Christmas once again. Mum and I have one more weekend away planned in December (to Filey of all places!) and then a pleasant family festive time to look forward to, so on that note I'll pull this account to a close and wish you all a Merry Christmas and a Happy New Year!

with love and best wishes for another year,

Mum and Dad

xxxxx

Dear Bairns,

Merry Christmas!

Our New Year celebration last year was another sign of the march of time – no children to be seen anywhere and us parents out around the pubs of Penistone! My birthday came along, was celebrated and duly went the way of all the others then your Mum and I set about planning our year long celebration for our 25th wedding anniversary. We had lots of plans and holiday ideas to cram into the twelve months ahead.

The day after my birthday I had a dental appointment at the apt old joke of a time of 2:30. Two days later it was all girls off out to look at wedding dresses – what a full year we had ahead of us.
So, as the wedding dress was chosen I sorted out my first treat – and what could be more fitting as a first treat? A new shed of course – what more can one ask for in the early days of January. After that we continued our ongoing difficulty with celebrating occasions appropriately that we have displayed over the years, but we might just have surpassed ourselves with Haggis for Chinese New Year and obviously a Chinese for Burn's Night...

Then it was James' birthday with a celebratory meal at Cubley Hall. A week later he was off to Austria with school for a skiing trip. Not sure how he got that and we got a week in the van at York (although Sue seemed to enjoy her night with Olly Murs which is perhaps some small consolation).

We didn't quite manage to do Pancake Day properly either. Due in small part (but not entirely) to the comings and goings of Hannah and her washing we had Pancake Day three times in a week to accommodate everyone.

In March I had good news and bad news at the optician – the good news was the eye sight test was on offer – the bad was I had to go in for a cataract operation!. With the money I saved on the test I treated us to a nice bottle of red...

Then it was up North to celebrate the birthday of Isabel's 'boyfriend' – wasn't sure what to expect at a 75th birthday party... It was a bit like being in an episode of Phoenix Nights...

We also decided to go to the cinema more often this year – went to see the Best Exotic Marigold Hotel at the paramount – we were about the youngest in there, so the 12A warning before the film started was a bit unnecessary. We've never had to queue to get out of a cinema before, some of those joints must have really seized up in the second part after the interval.
Still in March we got to St. David's day and I plumped for that famous Welsh dish, leek paella. Also, because I got too many leeks, the next night we had curried leek paella... But I managed to get it right for St Paddy – Guinness, Irish stew and Colcannon!

On Mother's Day I had to fill in at breakfast time in the absence of children, and also make the meal that evening and the pancakes for afters.... We did get down to the Huntsman for a nice pint in the middle of the day though.

At the beginning of April we had our first planned celebration; an excellent break in Prague. On the way there however we sat next to a Leo Sayer lookalike who was studying a number of books on the city which left me feeling very under prepared. So I asked the taxi driver for a couple of phrases on the way to the hotel – the two most useful were 'Dve piva prosim' (2 beers please), and Mum's favourite – 'Kde je zachod'? (Where's the toilet?).

Continuing our reckless approach to the year we had a weekend at Clumber Park in April – we even bought a heron and a salamander for the courtyard. A little later it was St George's day – celebrated with pasta obviously...and a week later Mum was off up another mountain in Wales with her girly gang.

When May arrived I found out as part of my studies that aboriginal people often employ indirect communication strategies. Shortly after that, Mum said one morning (as she left the kitchen heading for work);

'James will probably need that blue sheet...'

Me; what blue sheet

Mum; the one waiting to be washed

Me; so you want me to wash it?

Mum; but don't put it in the airing cupboard....

Who'd have guessed it, for 25 years I've been married to an aboriginal female!

I went for my op on the 10th of May, but they lost my notes so I came home, then they found so I went back...quite an eventful day. A week or so later it was the hen and stag weekend – and due to my implant I was banned from the Paintball. The girls set off for Manchester and the dubious delights of (C)Anal (S)Treat and we went off to York.

One week later it was our 25th Anniversary – rather than a party we opted to stay in and had a nice meal (six of us) and even sat out in the courtyard until around 11 p.m. We had also planned a weekend in the van to extend the event but Mum got a better offer and flew off to Crete with her friends... So James and I romantically celebrated the anniversary on the Go Ape ropes in the trees at Buxton. Still managed a few pints though (too many perhaps as I fell over racing James back to the caravan...)

June brought us our next planned celebration – combining Mum's birthday and a week in Scotland taking in the Isle of Skye, with Loch Lomond on the way and Glasgow on the way back.

Hannah decided that she might as well have a couple of celebrations as well so it was a Chinese to celebrate H_2O day and then off to a spa with sis and mum while James got to stand in the river Don for the weekend for his geography trip.

At the end of June came the wedding! Basically a three day long party (the first time I've ever been drank out of house and home...the shame of it...). Could have gone a bit wrong when Loz forgot to take her bouquet but as usual everything went fine on the day (days?).

We next dipped our toes into July and decided to buy a new car for Mum which we got just before we went off to France. St. Emilion this year – it doesn't get much better than being surrounded by over 1000 vineyards...

For our cycle weekend in August Mum and I combined our trip with a spa break – including my first time for a massage. Then another first we visited Chatsworth with the van.

A week later our next planned celebration arrived – a week in Ireland – car only and posh hotels – Dublin, Galway, Ring of Kerry, Killkenny. According to one road sign that we passed I happened to notice that it wasn't actually a long way to Tipperary... The highlight for me of course had to be the visit to Cong where they were serendipitously celebrating 60 years since The Quiet Man (probably the best film in the universe) was made – I even had a pint in Cohan's exactly where John Wayne did.

Immediately after that it was off to Leicester and then a cycle ride to Stratford and back....where I complained about my meal; got a better one and a free bottle of wine, as well as a nice chat in Spanish with the head waiter.

On 14 September we had another black day for the roads of Britain – James had his first driving lesson. How did it go? According to James, 'Awright....'

In October we attended a beer festival in Sheffield and Mum started to appreciate proper beers instead of that girlie lager stuff. A couple of days later we had another trip to the Paramount to see an amateur production of 'Allo 'Allo. It wasn't quite possible to suspend disbelief enough to see the young French maids in the gallant efforts of the ladies although Helga did her best...

As October drew to a close we had another trip in the van – this time to Bolton Abbey. While we enjoyed a week of walking, real ales and real fires in the pubs of Appletreewick we left James and our pumpkin at home to be pestered by little ghouls and goblins on Hallow'een. Then, with almost the whole year gone so quickly it was November. We still felt like throwing caution to the wind so we went out shopping and bought a few things for Christmas, mince pies and the like, and another impulse purchase of a car.... Well, according to you lot YOLO...

with love and best wishes for another year,

Mum and Dad
xxxxx

Dear Bairns,

Merry Christmas once more! Another year gone by and it's already time for me to write about the highlights of the year that was... 2013!

Yet again in 2012 we ended a year with a prophecy that the world was going to end. But as you can see it didn't (but of course one day they will get it right). Partly in celebration of our continued existence I decanted a 1960 Sandeman's port and I have to say that if the world had ended before I'd gotten around to that I'd have been incredibly disappointed not to have drunk it!

I spent my birthday at a place called Burn Hall with your mum and we enjoyed a pleasant walk along Sutton Bank before relaxing over a rather decent meal. On the way home the next day we fitted in another walk, this time around Newmillerdam Country Park before getting back to a family meal around the table.

Then, rather rashly perhaps, we put into place our belated New Year resolution (I can't see the point until after my birthday or I'm doomed to failure); to reduce the amount of bread we ate – and also to drink no alcohol until James' 18th birthday... This meant of course that toward the end of January we would be celebrating Burn's night without whisky. However I believe that I may have overcompensated for this by ordering 3kg of vegan haggis (which they managed to deliver from Scotland despite the snow).

Then came the big day – for James I mean not for us having a drink. He graded up to brown belt in karate and a day later graded up to an adult and the right to wear whatever belt he chose to. We celebrated with a pint in town (he ordered but I paid naturally...) and then a trip *en famille* that evening to an Indian restaurant.

A few days later we got the news that we were to become grand-parents and that just added to the pleasure of another family weekend away; this time in a cottage in Bonsall near Matlock Bath. It was great having the whole family around and going for walks in the snow and even better (or perhaps batter ⏺) the next day was Pancake Day.

But of course this started the great debate. Would it be granny Sue, grandma, nana... and what would I be called. My vote is for abuelito.

Completing his transition James also went on to pass his driving test later in February and then we rolled into the month of March and began planning our weekends (and longer breaks) away in the caravan. First stop was a week near Great Malvern which also incorporated St. Patrick's Day and a pre-prepared stew and colcannon with a few pints of the black stuff to wash it all down. We had an excellent time cycling and walking despite the cold and snow, and now of course it was just the two of us enjoying these times away, which set the scene for the months to come. Plenty of snow however also gave a little cause for concern – we weren't snowed in at the site but we were almost snowed out at home as it was so deep we could hardly get the caravan back to the house (thank goodness for children who can clear the drive in our absence).

April brought the first of many scan images of the awaited baby. Little did we know how photogenic she would become so soon (whether she wanted to be or not) – and later on how Facebook has changed the world we live in... That same month we went to a live 'gig' (OK, I admit that's a bit grand for an audience of about twenty and two musicians) in the cellar bar at the Old No7 pub and were quite impressed with the music. A few days later everyone went off to celebrate Ricky's birthday in Sheffield, bowling.

Then we went off to Ashbourne in the caravan where I spectacularly came off my bike and got covered in pig s*!*... (Thankfully the omnipresent facebook was around to record this for posterity ☺) But just to prove I'm not the only one with hearing challenge, just before I came off the bike I'd been saying to Mum, 'Look Sue; a hare,' to which she replied, 'A bear?' Now I'm sure that you know that the Peak District is not renowned as a habitat for bears...

St. Georges Day, that rather blandest of saint's days, arrived. As usual I struggled with deciding on a themed meal; in the end it was a toss up between which of Britain's national foods to eat – we could have gone for a curry of course but opted instead for chip butties.

As the weather improved we had a bit of work done to the house. Extra windows in two of your rooms gave a view over the garden and we had the en suite renewed and slightly enlarged. And so April drew to a close. Mum went on a girly weekend walking in Wales, James had a maths weekend near Whitby (at the impressively named Boggle Hall), and Hannah came home to borrow the car, I mean came home for a visit. I spent the weekend dodging hailstones while trying to improve the garden – the drawback of improving its visibility from the house.

For May Bank holiday we decided to brave Ashbourne again and thankfully I remained upright on my bike the whole time. We even managed a brief period of sitting outside in the sunshine until the cold wind forced us back into the shelter of the caravan.

A week later we left the cold behind and flew off to Corsica for a week. A truly beautiful place where we did loads of walking every day. We were staying near Ajaccio, the birthplace of Napoleon, and I was tempted to have a look around his house but he wasn't at home so it didn't seem appropriate.

When we got back home we celebrated our anniversary with a nice meal at the Wortley Arms before setting off on a cycling weekend which even took in a stopover at Stilton where thankfully it didn't smell of cheese. But incredibly it was yet another haunt of Dick Turpin. The man must have stayed in every pub in England! You would think that the wanted poster of the time would have been more effective if it mentioned, 'beware, this man often stays in hotels and regularly leaves without paying, leaving by a window with a shout of 'I must go, they are after me again...' And when we were initially overcharged when we checked out to the tune of £350 we thought he might have left a line of his descendants in charge of this particular hotel...

Then we took ourselves off in the caravan to Boroughbridge to cycle a bit more and celebrate mum's birthday. And what did we do the following weekend? We cycled down to Belper and back of course...

Which brings us nicely to another milestone birthday – Hannah's 21st. Quite a hectic weekend with every bed, and room, and even the caravan occupied on the drive; all topped off with a trip to Sheffield to play crazy golf.

The next week we headed off in the caravan once more, this time near York. We tried to do a few walks but almost every path in every direction had been blocked by farmers. Most frustrating...

But the week after that we were actually joined by James for a weekend at Delamere forest. I was so surprised I almost fell off my bike. Well actually I did fall off my bike but that's another story. And as soon as we got back it was a dash over to Manchester to see James fly off to Tenerife for a week.

Later in July I had a week in Santiago de Compostela (the week before the train crash), as part of my Spanish course. The weather was kind and helped to make the visit even more memorable.

When I got back it was another trip to drop off James yet again (only as far as school this time as it was a bus to London for the first leg of the trip). Then he was off on his trip to Malaysia – such a hard life he has for one so young...

While he was away we fitted in another long weekend, this time at Losehill, as we entered August. On this occasion we were joined by Ricky for the day and Loz stayed on for the night – far too complicated for the reception staff to handle though. And then it was off to France. Loads more cycling all around the local vineyards and chateaux and along the banks of the Loire – marvellous! A highlight had to be the visit to the Tin Tin exhibition, oh and the fantastic wine of course, which we obviously had to bring a sample or two of back home.

As usual September followed quickly on the heels of August, and soon it was the 9th of September and Tamzin increased the size of the family by an extra few pounds (6 and 12 oz in fact). And as she entered, a week later James left to go to university. And as he entered his first year Hannah entered her final year there. Luckily we'd had a few practice weekends without children so far this year because the house is really quiet with only the two of us in it.

Of course a new baby trumps a mother's birthday so Loz's birthday passed quite quietly this year.

Toward the end of September we also had a few nights near Newark and a bit more cycling around our old stomping ground down as far as Southwell and across to the river Trent. We even came close to buying a motorhome but thankfully common sense prevailed.

In October I sat my final exam in Spanish and the next day we flew off to Menorca where I thought I might be able to put it to use. But the entire place is basically one large tourist resort. It was like being in a warm and beautiful part of England where everyone was English apart from the waiters! And the number of walking sticks was incredible – we felt *really* young.

To celebrate Halloween we left Hannah in charge of giving out sweets to strange children while we spent the night at Sheffield theatre where we saw the marvellous Priscilla Queen of the Desert. And we didn't celebrate bonfire Night on the 5th either. Instead we sat outside on the 4th eating and drinking in front of a fire in the courtyard as I celebrated having survived mum closing the garage door on my head... And then it was off to the Lakes to celebrate M's 50th – three days of walking and a trip into Ambleside for a meal and the cinema. This was seven days into Movember and James and I had agreed to Ricky's suggestion of growing facial hair for the month – I opted for a goatee...

Toward the end of November I was even trusted with Tamzin on my own for the day. We had great fun of course, I read a book, and she ate, slept and cried for food or a change of nappy - but good gracious those nappies...

And a week later I got my results for my course and now I can apparently put BA(Open) after my name, so, just like the Scarecrow form Oz now that I've got a piece of paper I should be really fluent....

We left November and meandered into December with a weekend in a cottage near to Grassington in the Yorkshire Dales (where coincidentally there was a Dickensian fare – complete with unprotected braziers despite the large crowds!). All of which brings us full circle, back into December, almost the end of another year, and the saunter toward Christmas. Once again the family will gather around the tree singing carols and drinking mulled wine in festive jumpers with a broad smile on every face basking in mutual peace and goodwill.... yeah right!

with love and best wishes for another year,

Mum and Dad

xxxxx

Dear bairns,

So, 2014 eh? What better way to get the New Year off to a great start that a pint of Theakstons? Therefore, off we went to Masham for my birthday, a muddy walk, and two brewery visits. Later in January, Hannah decided to trump this with a visit to Rome.

Continuing our now customary lack of precision, we had Haggis the day after Burn's night and we even fitted in a trip over to Grimsby. However, I really excelled at a lack of precision when I turned up in Sheffield for a pint to find that I was a whole week early! James kindly saved the day by agreeing to meet his old dad for a pint...

At the end of January, we had a celebratory leak for Chinese New Year – no it wasn't St David's Day, it was a leak in the kitchen – just what I needed when preparing the Chinese. However, undeterred we battled on toward James' birthday which was a big Indian meal with everyone around for the evening followed by trivial pursuit until midnight.

Apparently being a bloke is no excuse for forgetting things like 'we got engaged on Valentine's Day 28 years ago'. So I tried to make up for it with a nice meal – homemade chocolate truffles with Prosecco in the bath (not actually in the bath of course...), then artichoke and garlic stuffed olive tartlets with asparagus followed by linguine topped with wild mushrooms. All accompanied with a nice Valpolicella Ripasso before we had chocolate pots and a glass of Marsala..... anyone feeling hungry yet?

In mid-February I added a few more letters behind my name when I finished my OU Degree and about the same time James decided his course wasn't any good and wanted to swap to aeronautical engineering. Not quite the same as accounting but we'll see what he makes of it.

But the highlight of February must be our trip to the concert at Leicester – The Ukulele Orchestra of Great Britain. And before you scoff look them up on youtube – they are great.

Into March and we planned for St. David's Day. I went shopping for the ingredients – and forgot to buy the leeks (thinking we might still have one in the kitchen⊡), so off I went back to the shop.

Had no problem at all though when it came to Pancake Day!

Later in March we got the first taste of the unseasonably mild year that was to come – it was a great weekend of cycling, walking, all the family around for lunch etc. Oh and the discovery of hundreds of unexploded ordinance, bullets, hand grenades etc. in a house around the corner – Sue was oblivious to the fact that she drove past the police cordon on the way to work.

The week after that we spent a week in the caravan at Threshfield near Grassington and rode some of the roads that the Tour de France would use later in the year. It rained almost the entire week but at least we squeezed in a St. Patrick's stew and colcannon with a drop of the black stuff.

To finish off a quite full March we all went off en famille to Sherwood Pines, the day after we had a log burner installed chez nous, for a few nights in a log cabin. Plenty of walking, games, meals, quizzes etc. and it was warm enough to enjoy the hot tub.

In April we took a break from repainting 'the reading room' after the mess of the log burner installation to go to the Paramount to watch a band called Talon. They were very good in our humble opinion. So, two weeks after it was installed we lit the first log fire – even if it was like a summer evening – we were determined.

In mid-April we fitted in a long weekend near York and some more cycling before we had another hectic weekend around Easter. Loz cooked us a curry on Good Friday, we were in Leicester on Saturday and on Monday we went to Sheffield to see Dirty Dancing at the Lyceum.

We celebrated St Georges Day with the customary curry then it was off for another van weekend at Clumber Park this time…. Followed in early May by another to Carsington Water.

After the excitement of the Eurovision Song contest – and I must say I sense a diminution of interest from certain family members… We flew to Madeira. Lots of new experiences there including perhaps the best – walking the lavadas (scary, high, narrow and with sheer drop on one side). We even went to a casino for the first time. Perhaps the most disappointing was finding out that the museum of electricity was closed on Sunday – I was looking forward to that. The most worrying (more so than the lavadas) was watching the plane do a 'u' turn to get enough distance to take off!

The day after our anniversary in May we got a call from Hannah who had just been in a car accident. Thankfully nothing serious but the shock of receiving a call is pretty extreme.

Quote of the week? Loz lost her phone and I found it later in the car. 'Ok', said someone who shall remain nameless, 'I'll text her to say we've found it'. ??????

Then it was Sue's 50th! So, despite a cold and a sore throat she set off for a girl's weekend at York races to feed her gambling habit that had been born in the casino. I even made a cake for when she got back – admittedly, it would have been better if I'd used baking powder like the recipe said and not bicarbonate of soda... The next day we went off to a place near Bakewell called Sheldon's Retreat to celebrate her actual birthday.

To coincide with the 70 year commemorations of D Day we set off to Kegworth (no real connection actually, just coincidence). This should have been our cycling weekend but Sue still had a sore throat so we had our first cycling weekend without bikes. When we got back home we noticed that we had a resident blackbird who's call had a terrible resemblance to the opening bars of 'I'm a Barbie girl', which, once heard you can't get out of your mind. Simultaneously Hannah proved she wasn't a Barbie girl and got a 2:1 for her dissertation!

We set off once again in the van – on Friday 13th June. We were lucky though, managing a walk and getting back before it rained. On the other hand I tripped over the hitch and hurt my leg, got a nettle sting, twisted my ankle, got a blister, and trapped my hand in a belt clip...but I did get my three texts for Father's Day while on a 6 hour walk around Mam Tor.

Hannah was 22 on the 22nd and we took full advantage of the great weather to make a weekend of it. Outside until midnight and a table for 10 at t'iamo for an Italian.

189

Another weekend slotted in at the end of June near Boroughbridge and some further cycling of roads to be used by the Tour. Most helpful sign on the route as we struggled uphill? 'Cheer up, the worst is yet to come!'

And then on the 5th and 6th of July the Tour de France came to Yorkshire! It was fantastic, we rode most of the local route (about 50 miles over a lot of climbs) and rode on roads closed to traffic, and watched the Tour ride by...I'm almost lost for words.

A week later we were in France –the year just kept getting better. Two weeks in the Loire valley and 321 miles covered on our bikes. Excellent!

We managed to make it to 1st August before another weekend in the van, this time we went to Chatsworth. Through the rest of August we fitted in trips to Leicester, Grimsby, and a picnic with Loz and Tamzin (including Sue's first visit to a bird hide) before going off again for a long bank holiday weekend to Rutland water.

At the end of August Ricky kindly volunteered to help Sue with the ice bucket challenge which I think he enjoyed a little too much, and that same weekend we managed to fit in our postponed cycling weekend. We cycled to the Boat Inn at Hayton, a round trip of 100 miles.

In early September we got to Bolton Abbey for four nights then it was Tamzin's 1st birthday (which we celebrated a week later with a family fun day and BBQ at Rother Valley).

The family all turned out in force again to celebrate Loz's birthday – nachos and quesadillas as requested. And a bit more babysitting duty as the girls celebrated in Sheffield.

A week later we spent another 4 nights away. Sheriff Hutton this time and a lot more cycling. Then we entered October – another full itinerary. We watched Ricky in his boxing match (he was robbed!), we watched Hannah drive off in her first car, and we played bingo in Ashington... on the way to a week of walking in the Cheviots.

And once again we managed almost a week before we were off again – this time to Belper – but at least we were home for Halloween. I carved two pumpkins this time and we had the pleasure of at least 70 darling children demanding sweets with menace (actually they were all really polite this year). To recover we went to the beer festival in Sheffield the next day – not knowing that we would be playing sardines on the train due to a local football match...

The next day we went to Sheffield again to buy a bike for sue and ironically the Giant (the brand) was too small, so they had to order in a larger size.

Only me, Sue and Hannah around the fire for bonfire night this year but we did our best. Sparklers, a few beers, and managed a whole loaf of bread toasted on the fire; not bad for three people.

November continued with a further flurry of visits, busy weekends etc. but there were two highlights. The first of course was Hannah's graduation, a 2:1 overall (followed by an excellent Mexican meal); and the other, almost as impressive, Sue clocked up her 1000th mile on a bike so far this year!

November rolled into December with a day trip over to Grimsby with Tamzin for a spot of gardening, more babysitting (a pleasure rather than a chore), Christmas shopping, more meals followed by a relaxing chat around the log fire... roll on Christmas I say. What a full year we've had, and I'm sure there's more to come!

with love and best wishes for another year,
Mum and Dad
xxxxx

Dear bairns,

Well another year is almost up – it seems to have gone faster than ever this time.

Not surprisingly the first event of the year was Dad's birthday, this time celebrated at Helmsley with a nice walk to Rievaulx Abbey and back. What was surprising was receiving two cards from S and best of all a stepdad card from James!

Later in the month we had a week in France without the caravan for a change. Started off badly with a chipped windscreen and then we tried to book into the wrong hotel – all this before we had even got to the tunnel. But after that it was great – staying in various Chateaux, trying lots of sparkling wine (and stocking up the boot for when we got home) – even finding good food to eat. Everything went great until we got back to Calais – delays meant that the journey home took 16 hours. The next day James popped in to say hi and to tell us he'd dropped out of Uni...

We also celebrated Burn's night again when we got back, with haggis and whiskey (yes we know whiskey is Irish and whisky is scotch – but Jamieson's is vegan). Then, the day after that a chap came to fix the windscreen.

'You've got a double impact' he said.

'I see...'

'Can't repair double impacts unless they are 100mm apart'.

'I see...'

'If it was single I could repair it'.

'I understand'

'Let me show you...'

'No, I really understand...'

He still showed Dad. Then he phoned the office. 'Hello,' intake of breath through teeth, 'it's a double impact...'

Where did we put that whiskey...

A few days later another chap arrived with the replacement screen. But when he looked at it he said, 'It's a double impact'......... But he went on to fix it.... apparently you can fix a double impact...

We next saw James again on his birthday. Relatively quiet affair starting with a trip to the pub to play bar billiards. Then we rounded off a nice day with an evening meal.

We had a cottage break in mid-February at Alston. Arrived to no heating or hot water so made do with a log fire instead. We went to Hadrian's Wall but only saw dense fog (bet the Roman's loved being stationed there). Also went to Haltwhistle and saw a plaque stating that it was the exact centre of Britain – but the whole town was shut so perhaps it is the dead centre. Back at the cottage we made up for it by celebrating Valentine's Day with a nice bottle of Gevry Chambertin.

Pancake Day this year coincided with National Chip week. However, given Hannah's repeated request for pancakes we ended up having Pancake Week – and we had Chip Day after going to the cinema to watch Kingsman. This led us nicely up to Chinese New Year – year of the goat apparently – prepared a meal for about eight as usual as Dad gets carried away – even though there was only three of us to eat it. And this year Mum made Welsh Cakes for us all when St. David's Day came around. A few days later it was national pie week – well if we must....

It was quite amusing going to the cinema to see the Second Best Exotic Marigold Hotel – old people laughing at being old (and that was just the audience). The irony continued when Dad broke his tooth on cous cous – how Mum laughed. Until she lost a filling a couple of days later – how Dad laughed...

Friday 13th of March saw us all off *en famille* for a cabin weekend at Darwin Forest. Food, bubbly, hot tub, competitions (including how to fold a blanket), quizzes (how many ears does Captain Kirk have? Three of course, left, right, and final frontier...). The following week was St. Paddy's Day – need we say more?

In March we had a week in Spain – taking in Seville, Cordoba, and Granada. Totalmente estupendo – but unseasonably cold unfortunately.

Easter fell at the beginning of April and saw our first outing in the van. Four days at Carsington cycling and walking. A week later we visited the nearby vineyard at Holmfirth. Couldn't tour the vines due to horizontal rain. Tasted the wines but couldn't buy any... only in England!

A couple of days later Dad went in for his second cataract to complete his double glazing and a week later we went off to Sheffield for the night followed the next day by a BBQ chez Loz and Ricky. April's events calendar terminated with St. George's and a spot of babysitting so we learned a little algebra;

St. George + curry = Wetherspoons.

Tamzin + babysitting = knackered!

May started with a trip to Pickering to watch the Tour of Yorkshire where we watched two stages; then it was back home to catch the final stage as it passed relatively near to us. Star Wars Day (May the 4th be with you) was celebrated by a spot of gardening, ably assisted by Tamzin. We got another weekend of cycling in after that at Buxton. For our anniversary we went to Moreton in Marsh – yet more cycling and walking.

Mum's birthday weekend started *en famille* with another meal around our table – Indian themed this time. Next day we went off to continue the celebrations with a stay at Fearby then back home for the actual big day. Another year and she still managed to watch a James Bond film through to the end!

This was followed by a weekend over near Newark and then Father's Day celebrated with a fire in the courtyard and James continued his confusion mission – this time coming home to celebrate - but leaving the card back in Sheffield! The next day he went home and came back with the card as it was Hannah's birthday – except instead of a Father's Day card he also gave Dad a Birthday Card – can't wait to see what he gets for Christmas.

Our trip to France was somewhat earlier than usual, getting there on the 27th of June just in time to enjoy two weeks of a heatwave. Lots of cycling and wine tasting of course... Once home we continued to cycle – down the trail to Wortley, up Holme Moss –

even bought a chariot for Tamzin so we can tow her along behind us.

Into August we had a weekend at Chatsworth, followed by another at Rutland, and a further break of five days near Grassington. All of this cycling was in part preparation for our cycling tour of Holland which we did at the beginning of September. We took the ferry from Hull (with bikes only) and had a great time despite some frustrating weather and visited Amsterdam, Den Helder, and Utrecht. When we got back it was Tamzin's second birthday. Co-incidentaly Hannah booked her flight to Vietnam that same day.

We managed to squeeze in an impromptu meal to celebrate Loz's birthday then we were off for the weekend again. This time we went to Belper and Mum clocked up her 1500th mile on the bike so far this year.

We got a long weekend in at Hope in October. Lots of walking this time but again some disappointing weather so the views weren't great – apart from one of the days when it was sunny and hot. The following weekend we started our Christmas shopping...

In mid October we went to church. Ok admittedly only because there was a beer festival on... but we still went to church. A few days later it was 'Back to the Future Day' – the date in the future in the film had arrived and not a hover board in sight. So now the future is in the past I suppose that is time travel? Halloween quickly followed (when did it become compulsory for Dad to do two pumpkin carvings?) - we went off to Sheffield to watch the Bodyguard but got back in time to dole out sweeties – Tamzin even went out dressed as a little witch.

Then of course it was Bonfire Night – and as you know Dad loves setting fire to things. We had a great night, undeterred by the occasional spot of rain. A couple of days after that we headed up to the Lakes for a week – never seen so much water in our life.

At the end of November we had our first of three Christmases this year when the outlaws turned up. As they will be in America on the actual day we planned a mini Christmas with all the trimmings. The second Christmas is scheduled for the weekend before Christmas - another weekend in a cabin at Darwin Forest (brought forward from next year so Hannah can come before jetting off in January), and the third one on, well the 25th December surprisingly.

And then that just leaves New Year before the whole cycle (and Mum's cycling) starts over again!

Lots of love and best wishes for another great year,

Mum and Dad

xxxxx

Dear bairns,

Well December is finally here once more, so time to look back over events of 2016!

We started the New Year by almost missing it – only just got the Champagne open in time. From then on time started moving quite quickly, setting the scene for the year ahead I suppose. A few days into January I celebrated my birthday (getting to the stage where the candles cost more than the cake) and a few days later it was a trip over to Manchester to drop off Hannah on her way to teach English in Viet Nam. Straight after that we had a nice long weekend of walking in Derbyshire before getting back to babysit while Loz had a scan – Tamzin is going to have a baby sister! So many things to celebrate this year.

Toward the end of the month we celebrated Burn's Night although with an Irish flavour as I don't have Scotch whisky. Had the haggis with colcannon this time just to further confuse things.

Then James had his 21st! A low key celebration before he went off to Utrecht for a nice break. The rest of February brought us up to Chinese New Year, followed by St. Valentine's and of course an extra day due to it being a leap year.

March followed with St David's day and what I'd like to think would evolve into a national dish – leek satay wrapped in chapatti with a wine and whiskey sauce.... On Mother's Day we celebrated with a 5k run just because we could.

A week later it was off to Lanzarote for some winter Sun. St Paddy's arrived while we were there but we refused to visit one of the Irish bars – it just isn't right. A nice relaxing break though, including walking just under 60 miles during the week.

Easter eased us gently over into April, and like Fool's we went off and bought a motor home. We did do our research for a change, we checked out at least two before deciding. April also brings daffodils. About ten years ago I put about 100 bulbs on the hill but hardly any ever bloom – this year we had 5 in flower – until Tamzin pulled the heads off a couple to give to grandma…

We managed a trip to Castleton mid-way through the month and later celebrated St George's by going to the first of numerous beer festivals. A week later we had a few days (a six day long weekend…) over at Carsington Water where we rode through snow, sleet, wind, blizzards and then the next minute being too warm – crazy weather!

A bit of culture in May – off to Leeds to see Flavia and Vincent in 'The Last Tango'. Then it was the Eurovision song contest – now I'm sorry but when did Australia qualify as being part of Europe???

Mid May and we had a normal day for once, out on the bikes with Tamzin in the chariot, then a spot of gardening, and a Skype call from Hannah saying she decided not to go travelling after Viet Nam because she was pregnant…

A week later we celebrated our wedding anniversary with a trip to Knaresborough – nice and romantic – another 60 miles on the bikes over the weekend.

May seemed to provide a pregnant pause for us to catch our breath – apart from a trip to Nostell Priory (or Nostril Priory as mum prefers to call it).

Then June arrived! Loz's due date came and went. Then, on mum's birthday, I went over to get Hannah from Manchester, James came home from the Netherlands, Loz, Ricky and Tamzin came over as well – and Loz decided she wanted an Indian takeaway. Ordered, delivered, and eaten.

Then, half way through watching the wedding singer mum had to drive them to the hospital; driven, no delivery, false alarm. The next morning after breakfast they had to detour to the hospital again on the way home; finally delivered (in record time!), Elodie, 6 lb 9 oz!

A week later, another trip to the airport, this time to pick up the new 'son-out-law' who not only arrived to meet us for the first time but as this also coincided with a visit from the outlaws (plus Loz, Ricky and the girls as it was a combined weekend of Father's day, Hannah's birthday etc.) he got almost the full in at the deep end treatment as soon as he arrived. Was Brexit a coincidence or linked to this arrival of the latest immigrant from Ireland?

Toward the end of June we went off (still in the van as the motorhome hadn't arrived) for a couple of weeks in France near La Tranche sur Mer. Good for beaches but poor cycling country. The day after we got back we finally picked up our motorhome, but it was a couple of weeks before we got away in her (she's called Fabuelos...) to a site near Newark, but this was quickly followed by another weekend to Chatsworth which tipped us into August.

August turned out to be a busy month as well including a visit to Leicester, James getting back from a three week tour around Europe, Hannah off to Ireland to meet Ryan's parents, Ricky and Tamzin off to Cyprus for a wedding, a trip to Bolton Abbey with Loz and Elodie in Fabuelos, and me finishing work for good.

In September we took Fabuelos over to France, the Netherlands and Belgium for week of cycling and visiting Bruges for a beer or two, plus the odd 130 miles of riding. When we got home, Holme Moss was visited – mum didn't do the ride but Ryan made it.

We then had a pleasant long weekend at Sandringham. Later that month, after Loz's birthday, Hannah and Ryan rented a house in Barnsley within waddling distance of the hospital and we got our house back! At the end of September we got away again for four nights to Moreton-in-Marsh.

When we got back it was October and James took over mum's car and became independent of public transport while we went down to one car. The rest of October went by just as fast as the other months. Trips to Ikea to replace the bed that Hannah took with her, decorating and rearranging the spare bedrooms, another beer festival in the church, followed by another in Sheffield and finally another trip in Fabuelos for Halloween.

Then of course it was bonfire night, then the boiler broke on the coldest night of the year so far, and the next day we had the first snowfall! Obviously this was quickly followed by the first log burner session of the year...

The remainder of November consisted of a number of ploys to get Hannah's baby to arrive. Various meals or varying degrees of spiciness, a trip to the sculpture park, even praying to the super moon – but her due date came and went with no baby. In frustration we went to another beer festival...

Then came the busiest week of the year – at one minute to midnight on the 25th November Lily Ava finally decided to grace us with her presence, weighing in at 9 lb 9 oz! Then it was a hectic week of trips back and forth to the hospital, to chez Hannah and Ryan, to the airport for Ryan's parents etc. etc. We celebrated with fizz, with a trip to the Hunstman, we even celebrated with James' 21 year old port.

Now we've arrived at December once again. There are plans to visit Christmas markets, the respective houses are in varying states of readiness for Christmas and everyone is looking forward to the festivities. We're looking at how to fit everyone around the table this year...

But as usual we'll manage, and it will be great, and we'll have another great year under our belts – if there's any room after Christmas dinner!

Lots of love and best wishes for another great year,

Mum and Dad

xxxxx

Dear bairns,

Well now! As we saw in the New Year of 2017 chez S&M you lot invaded Hannah and Ryan's house so we can safely say that the year seemed to be off to a good start; swiftly followed a few days later with a nice family birthday celebration for me – even though I chose to do the cooking! My birthday treat continued with a trip to Chatsworth and some nice wintry walks.

This being the year of our 30th Wedding Anniversary we had compiled a list of things we wanted to do and on Sunday 15th we ticked off our first 'challenge' – log burner on straight after breakfast (and kept alight all day) while me and Mum spent the entire day in our pjs.

We then went on to celebrate Burn's night in style – haggis stuffed mushrooms with potato and swede mash topped with a whisky sauce. Then, to beat that, we went to see 'Strictly on tour' live at Sheffield, which actually surpassed our expectations.

The weekend that followed was one of the most hectic of the year. Friday spent preparing the Chinese for the Chinese New Year. Saturday, everyone over to Grimsby to celebrate grandma's 80th (including playing pass the parcel with a multitude of her friends who did seem to enjoy a drink). Then everyone back home to eat and drink our way through Chinese New Year until 1 a.m. We still had to be up early for James and L's trip to Prague – and as we were in Leeds we just popped in to a shop and bought 2 new sofas on the way back to the car. Doesn't everyone?

One of our other challenges was to eat Italian for two weeks – didn't go too well – had a visit to York to see Gaslight and ate in a couple of vegan bistros before getting home to celebrate (belatedly) James' birthday – admittedly with pizza, but the next day we all had an Indian takeaway...

Mid February, mum and I went to the theatre to watch Ghost and the next day we all went to have a family photo shoot (organised by Loz and Ricky) followed by a trip to Cubley on the way home. Then of course came Valentine's Day – staying in for a nice meal but we then watched a quite depressing film called Le weekend – can't recommend it lowly enough. The following weekend Mum and I went off for the weekend of camping at Lickpenny in Derbyshire where we walked, cycled, celebrated National Drink Wine day, and finally had our fourteenth Italian day (only took us three weeks to do our fortnight...). At the end of the month we had pancakes for breakfast, pancakes for tea, and still had some batter left over – Pancake Day should really be two days I think. Immediately afterwards we had welsh cakes and leek tartlets for St. David's Day. In early March we all went on our annual cottaging experience – this time complete with great grandma and grandad. As usual it was an exhausting weekend of relaxation. The following weekend Mum and I went for a relaxing weekend on our own which involved muddy walks around Castleton and climbing Win Hill. We did our best to celebrate national pie week, managing two or three over the course of the week. The following week saw us having a Ryan led celebration of St. Patrick's Day. I didn't even have to cook this time, plus I won the 'Irish for a Day' quiz. The day after we set of for some winter sun on Gran Canaria where we had a great time. For Easter we managed to combine a beer festival at the White Heart with the usual egg hunt (for Tamzin mainly as Elodie a bit young and Lily on a trip to Ireland). A week later we took Tamzin with us for a weekend to Clumber Park and on our return celebrated St. George's with curry and chips!

During the following week we went to the funeral of Grandma's sister and at the same time Grandma's health took a turn for the worse. After that it was back and forth to Grimsby for appointments and then hospital as the news kept getting worse. In the midst of this we celebrated our 30th Wedding Anniversary before setting off for a long weekend in Rome while Karen was here to be with Grandma and Grandad. The celebrations continued for Mum when we celebrated her birthday with a nice Italian meal and a trip so see 'Kevin and Karen dance'.

June was also quite hectic. James went off to visit Viet Nam, Karen's family came over from America, we had a celebration party for Grandma in her garden with lots of her friends and family and we also celebrated Hannah's birthday.

During July we continued our trips over to Grimsby (although I did also manage to walk two of the three peaks one weekend with James) and at the end of the month we all managed a weekend away at Scarborough camping before making some room in our house ready for Loz, Ricky, Tamzin and Elodie to move back in while their new house is built.

August was a bit of a blur. We managed to keep Grandma at home until it was decided that she would benefit more from going to the hospice where they did a great job of stabilising her. She passed away there, peacefully, on the 10th and the funeral took place one week later.

After that mum and I managed a weekend away at Rutland water before going back to Grimsby to help sort out Grandad's moving into a care home at Waltham. Meanwhile Loz et all moved in and a week later so did James (only for a couple of months between flats). Mum and Karen managed to fit in a well deserved spa break toward the end of the month before Karen returned to America.

At the beginning of September Mum and I went for a weekend to Hawkshead in the Lakes and had a full weekend of walking, staying at a vegan B&B and going to vegan restaurants in the evening. Just what we needed to recharge our batteries.

We celebrated Tamzin's birthday a day late then Mum and I went to Moreton-in-Marsh for another weekend of cycling, walking, good food and a trip to Hook Norton brewery! The rain was very kind to us – only raining when we were in a pub or restaurant.

Loz had a quiet birthday but then went to see 'Grease' which she enjoyed. Then Mum and I went off on a belated holiday to Bruges and then Luxembourg during which we became quite the connoisseurs of Belgian beers, especially Trappist ones. We also managed to cycle into Germany a couple of times.

Into October we tried our best with National Curry Week – we had at least four. Another trip to visit Grandad was followed by a short weekend at Tuxford and a cycle ride over to Lincoln and back. When we got back I decided it was now or never for my annual Holme

Moss challenge so off I went into the rain and fog and headwind. Almost didn't make it.

As the month drew to a close we spent three nights at Rutland Water coming back in time to provide the local children with lots of sweets. Almost missed them though as we spent the day helping James move into his new flat. Then it was bonfire night. I'd had so little opportunity for fires this year (OK, we'll ignore Grandad's shed... and the firemen – which Ricky missed unfortunately...) so I lit two. We had soup and snacks and sparklers and toast on the open fire with the whole family. The following weekend we had a Belgian Beer Tasting evening with eleven different beers (complete with tasting notes, and a scoring system!).

The next morning, despite varying degrees of after effect, most of us did the 5K Park Run over at Locke Park. Following this up with a large breakfast at Wetherspoons managed to settle any remaining rebellious headaches and at the same time undo all the good we'd achieved by running.

Toward the end of November most of us took turns to welcome the first bug of the season (feeling cold and nauseous but being hot etc.) but it didn't dampen the celebration of Lily's first birthday which went off really well.

Now we are into December, we've done our annual trip to Bradfield Brewery to stock up on Christmas drinks, the bairns have been to see Santa at Wentworth Garden Centre and in a couple of weeks it'll be Christmas day once again. It seems to be starting even earlier this year with most of the street already decorated inside and out and us coming under pressure to get the tree up sooner than we usually would.... Well we'll just have to see....

Anyway, that's our news from another year so it just remains to say, Merry Christmas and hoping that you have a Happy New Year,

Lots of love and best wishes for another great year,

Mum and Dad

xxxxx

Dear bairns,

What a hectic year!

It started off with a family gathering to see in the New Year and was followed immediately by dad's birthday at Brewer's Cottage behind the New Inn at Copston. Bar, restaurant and a brewery – what more could one ask! A week later we went off in Fabuelos for the weekend but when we got back it was so icy that we needed a push from the neighbours to get back onto the drive.

We celebrated Burns night with haggis as we always do and then it was off to Leeds to see Strictly Live. Great night despite initially booking the wrong hotel, losing the non refundable fee and then booking a disabled room at the correct hotel.

James' birthday in February was a home made curry – we suppose it would be called an Indian/Chinese fusion if we were posh. No time to rest though as we were up at 4 am the next morning to take James to the airport.

The following day we found the new micro pub in Oxpring and wandered in for a drink. Everyone seemed friendly and also seemed to know each other. It was packed. We realised why when we worked out that we had crashed a birthday party.

Then it was up to the Lake District for a week near Bowness where we were joined a couple of times by Hannah, Ryan and Lily as they were up there at the same time. We walked into Ambleside one day and planned to get the bus back to the site. We watched one leave as we checked the timetable, then walked a half hour along the route to get the next one a few stops on, stopped to take a photo and managed a photo of the next one going by in the background. Then we got soaked as two cars drove through a puddle at high speed.

At Windermere the following day we were so busy finding the right money for the toilets that we both ended up going into the wrong ones! After that it was rain, sleet and snow, and flooding. But as Mum says we are always lucky with the weather.

Back home again it was time for Chinese New Year – this time cooked for everyone by Hannah and Ryan. The next day was national drink wine day so it would have been a shame not to. We didn't really get to celebrate St. David's day as, due to the continued snow, the shelves were bare – not a leek to be found. We managed to conjure up some welsh cakes though.

Then, because it was cold presumably mum put the house up for sale. All rather sudden in the end. So to celebrate we went off to Delamere Forest for the weekend.

We didn't quite manage to give St Patrick his due either this year as we set off to Fuertaventura that day. We had a great time and discovered two things about the island apart from how windy it is (hence its name), The first was that it is full of Italians. The second that it has loads of vegan bistros!

While we were there we sold our house, found out that the one we wanted to buy had already sold, and then spent days trying to arrange viewings for when we got back.

We returned home in time for Easter and a family dinner then we set off on a round of house viewings over the following week or so.

A week later we were off in Fabuelos again and had our offer accepted for our new house. As planned we downsized to a bigger place...

While we lazed about Ryan and Ricky both completed a half marathon in very respectable times.

Another week went by and then we went to see Aljaz and Janette work their way through some of Fred Astaire's routines.

Then it was St George's day. As it is now traditional to eat English meals to celebrate we continued the tradition with a nice curry as we have for some years now. But to modify it we had curry pie, chips, mushy peas and a bottle of Newcastle Brown Ale!

The following weekend it was the turn of Hannah and Ryan to start the house moving activities for this year. Hannah womanfully drove the van while the chaps did the lifting.

When May came around the corner it brought with it a lovely spell of hot sunny weather, just in time for Naked gardening day in fact. What could beat that you ask – Eurovision song contest we reply!

And another weekend in Fabuelos of course – this time to Carsington Water. After that it was our wedding anniversary. Champagne then a curry – we know how to live. We did celebrate further though with a nice weekend away at Sherriff Hutton – which unfortunately meant we wouldn't be able to help Loz and Ricky to move into their new house

Mums birthday was made into a long weekend of meals and lovely weather. In fact it went on so long it almost bumped into Ryan's birthday.

Loz, Ricky and the girls came over for Father's Day but Hannah was on a hen weekend and James was on holiday in Cornwall.

Then it was time for us to go off to France. Back to the Loire again. Wine tasting, lots of cycling, and even managed to see the vintage cycle rides which is a great spectacle. Even managed to find another mushroom museum. Unfortunately we didn't get to visit because it rained.

After getting back home we finally got a completion date of 19th July. To celebrate we bought a new motorhome and called her Fab Dos.

On the 18th we helped James move up to Leeds then on the 19th we moved ourselves. But not wanting things too easy we then went for a family camping weekend to Bakewell the very next day.

The rest of the very hot summer was taken up sorting out the house and garden, including numerous visits to the not so local tip and a visit from Karen. We made the most of every opportunity to get away in Fab Dos as well including a weekend down at Rutland Water. Loz and Ricky had their housewarming on the 20th August and a week later we spent the bank holiday weekend choosing wardrobes for our bedroom.

The following weekend it was everyone over here for the night after visiting Leicester for S&M's anniversary, then a week later it was our housewarming...

In September we got off again for a weekend at Bolton Abbey. A great time but one shouldn't rely on sat nav! Then, later in the month we set off for Gran Canaria for some early winter sun.

Lots of things around the house seemed determined to overlap or coincide or indeed arrange themselves back to front. Furniture arrived before carpets were laid. Oil was delivered at the same time as furniture. The fence had to be dismantled to move the oil tank. The electrics needed doing at the same time as the new bathroom was fitted etc. etc.

So as October came along so did the autumnal weather. We visited Knaresborough for the weekend and were glad we had left our bikes at home. Then it was another trip down to Leicester to watch the Calendar Girls at the theatre. Even got to taste a bottle of English Trappist beer brewed by the monks at St Bernard's Abbey. The following week, while picking up Lily after she had performed her duties as a flowergirl, we managed to block the vicar's car in and he was in a hurry to get off on holiday. As a thankyou Hannah and Ryan invited us for Sunday lunch but as they were worse for wear after the wedding festivities guess who ended up having to cook again...

No one around here does anything for Halloween so it was the first time for ages that we didn't even have a pumpkin carved.

Into November we had a great weekend away with the whole family at Woodhall Spa. Not one but two hot tubs! But once again, when we got back it was strange to have a Bonfire Night with no bonfire. Can't remember the last time that happened. But we did celebrate James' housewarming the next weekend over at Leeds and one week later we had a long weekend in Fab Dos at Peterborough.

So, as November gives way to December you can see that dad was right. You can't get much more hectic than every member of the family moving house in the same year. Of course we have downsized to a bigger place where once again it is difficult to find vegan places to eat – just as Barnsley has reinvented itself as the vegan capital of South Yorkshire.

And what do we have to look forward to in December. Well we have another family Christmas to look forward to. Except this year Loz and Ricky are hosting his family so we won't all be together on the day – but we will be at the pre Christmas bash at Hannah and

Ryan's. And then of course there will be New Year – hopefully complete with a newly installed log burner to add the finishing touches to our new home.

So there we are, another year has come and gone, so it only remains to say,

Lots of love and best wishes for another great year,

Mum and Dad

xxxxx

Dear bairns,

Well, it's beginning to look a lot like Christmas… so it must be time for me to write a condensed 2019 once again.

We saw the New Year in with a few drinks and made it to 3 a.m. before heading off to bed with the usual resolution to start a diet and drink less – from tomorrow!

Dad celebrated his birthday at Castleton where we were joined by Loz, Ricky, Tamzin and Elodie for a wander up Mam Tor. Tamzin did impressively and poor Elodie found the cold too much as she was in a child carrier. During the rest of January we continued to make minor improvements to the house. Cupboards fitted in the utility and we also bought a static bike (static as in it hardly moves…) Toward the end of the month we had a nice break with friends at Kilconquer Castle north of Edinburgh with the added bonus of dropping in to see K&Y on the way back.

In February we went up to Leeds to celebrate James' birthday at a restaurant with too much vegan choice. Then it was Chinese New Year which we celebrated in our bar. A trip to Knaresborough followed and then a nice meal in for Valentine's Day. As the rest of the month was quite mild we managed to explore more of our local area and found some nice walks. Also added four fruit trees to the garden. In fact toward the end of the month the hottest February days on record were recorded.

At the beginning of March James popped in and managed to share some of the Welsh Cakes made for St. David's day (leek and pasta bake this time). The next day we braved the club – Elvis night. The impersonator didn't. Undeterred, when James got back from Nottingham, we decided to try again as it was quiz night. It hadn't improved overnight.

Thank goodness for pancake day to help erase the memory.

March also brought more work on the house – or more accurately the garden. We got quotes for the patio and a new drive. While we decided which company to use we diverted ourselves by celebrating

St. Patrick's Day at Hannah and Ryan's where the family found out that Hannah was in the family way again. We then fitted in a trip to Graffam Water before getting down to a weekend of gardening and trying out the bikes we bought for our summer adventure. Toward the end of March we had a trip over to babysit the three girls and then celebrated Mother's Day with too much food at 'Church, Temple of Fun'.

April saw the work start on the patio and drive. I moved Fab Dos to help them with access, and immediately reversed into the house! After that we decided to put her onto a nearby campsite for the duration of the work. We also managed a night at Brownhills with entertainment from a singing group that did wartime songs and then a dance exhibition by some Strictly professionals. We also got to visit Melton Mowbray for the weekend. With the patio and drive finished we took advantage of the continued good weather and had a family get together over Easter (apart from James who was off around Europe).

In May we started painting the fence panels and installed a small shed to help with the storage in the garden. Then we had a weekend at Ferry Meadows, managing to walk in to Peterborough where we had our first visit to Subway ever. Next item was some repairs to the roof and further purchases for the Garden.

We were well and truly into countdown mode for Mum's retirement and took advantage of her leaving do being in Sheffield by staying over and having a nice meal. We then went back to babysit for Loz and binged on the Walking Dead until midnight! Thursday 23rd May was Mum's last working day as she had some leave to take up to her retirement date. We celebrated with some Moet, presents, and voting in the European elections...

Sunday 2nd June was the culmination of a great family weekend as well as being Mum's birthday and her official retirement date. Then it was packing and checking ready for our Grand Tour of Europe! We set off on Monday 3rd June. We visited France; Calais, Saumur, St. Emillion then moved on to Spain; Santander, Santiago de Compostela, Soutomaior then on to Porto in Portugal (got lots of presents for Father's Day while we were there), before crossing

Spain again; near Madrid, San Carles de Rapita, (happy birthday Hannah) and a Catalan site that seemed to be a fly sanctuary. Back into France; Montpelier, Antibes and Aigues Mortes in the Carmargue plus a visit to Chat. Neuf du Pape before moving on to Italy; Lake Como then the Stevoli pass (do not attempt in a motorhome) before getting to Germany; Augsburg. Back into France; Strasburg, Joinville, Calais. Then back home exactly one year after we moved in on 19th July having covered 4,302.1 miles.

Early August was marked by a family patio laying BBQ at Hannah and Ryan's then Loz and Ricky took the bairns off to Portugal following which Hannah and Ryan took Lily over to Ireland. So all in all no time for a family camp trip this summer. We did manage a break in Fab Dos with Tamzin though. Next home improvement concerned quotes for a new roof on the conservatory...

Toward the end of August and into September we had a mini tour of Scotland; via Ashington, Bamburgh, Cove, Forfar, Aberdeen, Culloden Moor, Inverness, Alloa, Melrose, Barnard Castle.

The rest of September saw us babysitting Lily, multiple visits to Grimsby, back over to Barnsley for Loz's birthday and secret party when she didn't get a lizard but did have a hired pizza oven then we had a trip away in Fab dos including a disappointing visit to Wychwood Brewery.

We spent the first couple of weeks of October chasing winter sun down on Gran Canaria

And we fitted in another trip to Castleton when we got back. Then it was time to have the new roof fitted to the conservatory. While they did that we decorated a room for the impending return of James prior to his planned travels next year. We then rounded off the month going to see Pricilla Queen of the desert at Leicester – an excellent production.

The work on the conservatory was finished on time and we set to painting the walls and ceiling. We ordered blinds and when everything was finished the place looked like a proper room.

James had invited us to go for a walk on Ilkley moor – but the day we agreed on was one of the wettest on record with a month of rain in one day. When Hannah et al came for a weekend she mentioned that we had 'visitors' in the loft. All part of living next to fields of course but now Mum has me setting humane traps and electronic deterrents all over the house.

We started painting the study only to find that it was really suffering from damp. So we got more quotes for more work that we couldn't afford not to have done. On a positive Loz won more than £3k at bingo.

Then of course came the new arrival –after keeping everyone waiting, James Joseph arrived with help, on Lily's birthday!

After a weekend of waiting and babysitting and a couple of visits to see our new grandson we had to dash back home to create chaos with the furniture so that the work could be done to rectify the damp. More decorating to do on the run up to Christmas!

But now December is here and the house is back to some semblance of order. In a week's time of course James is moving back before he goes off on his travels next year but hopefully that will just be organised chaos instead of the real thing. We've also got our pre-Christmas family get together to look forward to, courtesy of Loz and Ricky this year, and we will see everyone at some point or other here at Christmas time before we celebrate New Year and head toward a family weekend to celebrate dad's big birthday!

Lots of love and best wishes for another great year,

Mum and Dad

xxxxx

Dear Bairns,

So. 2020! What a year this has been!

It started off OK with the New Year seen in by a blocked drain and backed up toilet which was sorted by a rather valiant joint effort. If only the later restriction in toilet paper supply had been in place then...

Then it was off to Gisburn to celebrate Dad's 60th, another great family occasion which was followed by a few days up in the Lakes at Ambleside Manor with S & M. Shortly after we got back we took James over to L's and then they were off to New Zealand.

Toward the end of January we fitted in our usual celebrations but this year Burn's Night and Chinese New Year were on the same day. What a dilemma – even Dad drew the line at sweet and sour haggis. Although now that he thinks of it....

We wandered through to February and noticed that James wasn't in the country when it came to his birthday and two days later we weren't either as we headed off to Spain. We broke the journey into stages on the way down and eventually got to Moncofa on the 10th of the month. We were amazed by the first orange tree we saw – until we saw the mile upon mile of orange groves. It was a lovely holiday, lots of cycling and walking. We joined in a bit with the on site activities and even learned how to play whist.

The situation with Covid pretty much passed us by while we were there and only became real on the journey home when restrictions started, toilet rolls became scarce, and parts of Spain and France began to lock down.

By March however we were used to the overuse of 2020 vocabulary such as 'unprecedented', 'self isolation', 'social distancing', 'rule of six'... So, no family visits, no pubs, no restaurants – and it was about the last time we used real money! With March and April basically cancelled Dad decided to cancel his usual celebration of St. George's Day in protest.

He doesn't think anyone noticed...

We avoided shops but did lots of walking and cycling and even joined the Joe Wicks p.e. lessons.

In May we celebrated VE Day on our own in the garden with a few drinks and posh sandwiches. At least the lack of option let us spend lots of time in the garden this year.

As everyone's confusion increased when the message changed from 'stay at home' to 'stay alert', we continued to meet as a family virtually for a quiz – here in England with a drink and in New Zealand with a wake up cup of coffee.

By the end of the month Dad had organised all of the nuts, bolts, screws and nails in the garage by size, type, colour etc. No boredom here... Gave up on Joe Wick's – his back was killing him. But the garage is really tidy.

Our 33rd anniversary was just the two of us but we still had champagne and a nice meal. Home-made card this year as Dad didn't get to the shops.

The weather continued to be glorious as we reached Mum's birthday. Dad was a bit tired so he relaxed by laying a new base for a shed, relaid a path, moved the compost bins...

Hannah brought La-La and JJ over for Mum's birthday and the weather was kind again – against the rules to meet indoors, presumably one breathes vertically outdoors and horizontally indoors?

Anyway, the cakes, cookies, quesadillas and champagne went down well.

A couple of days later we managed to get over to Barnsley for Elodie's birthday and meet up with everyone who was still in the country – another great get together – as it was later when they came over here for a kind of early birthday do for Hannah and an early Father's Day.

Making the most of it we went over to Barnsley and joined Loz and Hannah and the bairns for a nice walk then on for a meal at Hannah's for her actual birthday.

Then Mum started having ideas that painting and decorating would be a good idea.

As July approached so did further restrictions but after Hannah bought a folding camper we planned a break for later in the month to Bakewell. We managed to fit in a trip to Peterborough earlier where it rained every day and we watched all three Pitch Perfect films on consecutive nights.

At the end of July we managed to get away again, despite the ongoing restriction, this time to Broadway in the Cotswolds which we followed with a trip to Rutland Water at the beginning of July. Then it was off to Leyburn for a nice walking holiday. Again we were lucky enough to see most of the family at different times in the month. On bank holiday Monday we were looking after Tamzin and Elodie and there was a country and western event on the field opposite which the girls enjoyed as we sat on the drive and enjoyed the day.

No France for us this year for obvious reasons but at the beginning of September we set off for our trip to the Isle of White and then the New Forest. We even managed to catch up with M, R and their new baby - F. In the absence of vineyard visits we switched to breweries. The bar is well stocked but no one can come over to help drink it all. Ah well... if Dad must...

Later in September we fitted in a visit to Barnsley babysit Tamzin & Elodie whilst Lauren & Ricky were going camping (this didn't happen in the end due to weather). Also, due to the 'rule of six' of course we could only get together sequentially, and when we went to Hannah's with the bairns that would have made eight – so Dad and Ryan went to the pub while Mum and Hannah enjoyed some peace and quiet with the four bairns.

Then, to emphasise the progress of the seasons, the weather changed and became very autumnal as the month came to an end. So, as the nights began to draw in Dad decided to learn Dutch (because French, Spanish and Italian isn't enough of course). Ik ben een appel.

And we went off to Buxton for a few nights where, surprisingly, we walked for miles and it rained all of the way.

After that we went up to Grassington for a few nights where, surprisingly, we walked for miles and it rained every day. But we also watched the complete series of Harry Potter films (apart from one – but we did have the empty case).

And that was October – another year without carving a pumpkin and another month of lock down about to be announced.

Which they did, to coincide with Bonfire night. So we sat in the garden around the brazier, drank soup, had a few beers, and ended up with some toast on the embers. And as the rest of November was cancelled so we did more walking and painting... At least in New Zealand James and L are managing to do some touring at last.

December went from a pleasant expectation of a few days family get together over Christmas down to 'visit on the day and do not sty over'. Bah humbug!!!As this is written there is a lot of uncertainty around January as well... They have invented tier 4 and the expectation is another national lock down. Next year? Who knows?

Lots of love and best wishes for another year as great as this (all things considered of course),

Mum and Dad

xxxxx

Dear Bairns,

Another year come and gone. It seems like time is speeding up!
But isn't technology amazing? At New Year we managed a chat with
Barbara up north, S&M in Leicester, Karen in the US, played a game
together as a family, and chatted to James in New Zealand!
Lockdown would have been a lot more frustrating without being
able to virtually get together. But it still wasn't the same as getting
together and celebrating in person.

Dad's birthday was on Monday this year. He used to hate that when
he was at work; but of course now it makes no difference at all. We
had to wait in though as we were expecting Mum's new phone to
be delivered – who's birthday was it again?

And the next day we went back into lock down again. So we
decided to go for a walk every day... which pretty much summed up
January, apart from a trip over to see granddad when visiting was
allowed.

We started to record our miles walked and signed up to do a 1000
mile challenge.

As usual we had haggis and trimmings for Burn's night. Then, as
January ended we nipped over to pick up James when he arrived
home from his trip to New Zealand. We reached 200 miles and
rewarded ourselves with chips and curry sauce!

We celebrated James' 26th birthday with a Mexican theme and sat
in front of the log burner with a G&T.

The next day they came to insulate the loft. We were in the kitchen
when James quietly observed that there probably shouldn't be a
pair of legs dangling through the ceiling above the dining table. We
all had a look as we sipped our tea, agreed with him, then called the
ambulance.

On the 11th of February we were called by the care home to say that
granddad was worse but we got another call 10 minutes later to say
that he had gone. At least Sue and James had been able to visit the
day before.

The rest of February was a bit up and down. Obviously we had things to sort out after granddad passed and we all went over to Grimsby for the funeral which of course was with restricted attendance and social distance in place. Mum did great with the eulogy and the coffin was carried by dad, James, Ricky and Ryan.

A week later James had moved out but it had been nice to have him home again for a while, including being able to celebrate Chinese New Year and pancake day – perhaps less so when celebrating Valentine's...

But he missed out on St David's – Mum's welsh cakes and a leek tart for tea.

We also had our first covid jabs this month. A day after mine we got to the 400 mile milestone. Celebrated by moving the compost bins...

Again thanks to technology Mother's day was a bit virtual this year, followed by a virtual St. Patrick's day but with real Guinness and stew of course. Three days later we achieved 500 miles. 500 more and we can lay down at your door.

The 26th of March was quite exciting – we had our first ever Costa drive through!

As the restrictions started to relax we did manage to meet up with you again but still not all at the same time. By the second half of April we managed to get out again in FabDos for a week at Sandringham. We cycled for miles in the unseasonably warm weather and saw more hares and other wildlife (such as muntjac deer) than we have ever done before. We got back home in time to celebrate St. Georges Day.

At the start of May we hit the 700 mile milestone.

We were in FabDos down at Peterborough on Star Wars Day before coming home and dropping her off for some work at the dealership. The 20th of May marked 10 calendar years since Dad retired from the NHS. A couple of days later we were off south to holiday in Somerset, Land's End and then meet up with Loz, Ricky and the bairns for a week near St. Austell. Probably skip over Mum's trip to A&E with a head injury... Nice way (not) to celebrate her birthday. Despite this we still managed to visit The Eden Project, The Lost

Gardens (quite easy to find actually – lots of signposts...) and Cheddar Gorge on the way home. We even popped in to visit The Jamaica Inn. During this break we also managed to catch up with M, R and F. Almost managed to catch up with S but it wasn't to be.

A mini heatwave in the middle of June also brought Hannah, Ryan and the bairns plus James for the weekend. We spent the rest of the month building our pergola in the garden and laying out some new paths.

The pergola was completed in time to celebrate (belatedly) Hannah's birthday and we had planned a whole family occasion but Covid struck again to prevent Loz making it over.

At the end of the month, in the continuing excellent weather, we set off for a break with S&M to the Lakes and incorporated cycle rides as well as climbing 'The Old Man of Coniston' and others over the Yewdale fells.

After Coniston we moved on to visit Hawes then Grassington before heading back over to Leyburn where we were joined by the whole family for a visit to The Forbidden Corner.

Toward the end of July Dad had a visit to Newark Hospital to see about his knee. The GP had referred him to physio for assessment. The physio referred him to a specialist (the one at the hospital) physio for assessment. This physio referred him to... physio.

A day later, proud to say that Loz (and Ricky of course...) completed the 'Tough Mudder'.

At the beginning of August we went to a campsite as part of a rally of the old people who we had met at Moncofa in Spain just before covid arrived. Surprisingly they were all a bit older than we remembered them. So we spent our days cycling. Wisbech sounded nice – but it wasn't.

A week after we got back we went to the Vegan Campout on the Newark showground. Dad enjoyed it.

August bank holiday gave us another family get together but this time it was James who couldn't make it.

Basically all of September was our tour of Scotland in FabDos. Up through Yorkshire and west of Edinburgh to visit Perth, Scone, Dingwall (where we made 1000 miles), Orkney, John O'Groats (so we went to both ends in one year), Granttown on Spey, Aberdeen (visit to the Gordon Highlanders Museum),Melrose and back via Haltwhistle and Richmond. During our trip we didn't see any whales or dolphins. We did see seals, a man cycling on a penny farthing, and a woman wearing full kimono etc. for no apparent reason. Having had such a good month we thought 'why not buy a new car?'. So we did.

However, having learned from our previous experience when we always bought the first one we saw, this time we didn't. We bought the second one.

We also managed to fit in some pumpkin picking in mid October but unfortunately ours went bad before we could carve it.

Then we went off for a five day break in FabDos near Grantham where it rained every day. All day.

Halloween was a family occasion over at chez Loz followed by bonfire night chez us (but Loz couldn't make it). Then we were off for some winter sun (and warmth) for two weeks on Gran Canaria. Bit of a shock when we got back, having left sun and 25 degrees to find East Midlands covered in snow and the temperature being minus 3!

To top it off we then got 'pinged' and had to do a PCR...

So now we are almost a week into December. We are now booster jabbed, off to babysit Tamzin and Elodie for a few nights, hopefully see everyone while we are there, then it will be the countdown to Christmas (at Hannah's then Boxing Day at Loz's) before dashing back to sort out FabDos ready to celebrate New Year down at Moreton in the Marsh.

And we still haven't managed to get to the Christmas market at Chatsworth. But who knows what next year will bring?

Lots of love and best wishes for another year as great as this (all things considered of course),

Mum and Dad

xxxxx

Part Five

The life of Reilly

Childhood memories of
the.real.ed.reilly

(and don't forget to add your own someday)

I was born in a council house on Chillingham Crescent, Ashington, but I don't really remember that of course and as we moved home soon after my birth I have no real recollection of it. Naturally I've seen the house, I passed it on the way to school. It was one of the houses that followed the curve of the railway that passed along the bottom of the garden where Dad apparently had grown strawberries and vegetables.

The trains still ran along the line from the pits until I was a teenager, dragging long lines of wagons loaded high with coal. Those of Mam and Dad's generation still recalled when the line also went down to Newbiggin running a passenger service.

The line bisected the town and the population were known by which side 'across the line' they lived – even the shops on the high street had a different feel depending on whether or not they were 'over the bridge'. Often in our school years we were tempted to race across when the barriers came down but usually we would content ourselves with waiting and waving at the guard as the last carriage rolled past.

As was usual in those days mine was a home birth. I was born with a 'veil' over my face ('en caul') and big enough to be famous for a day (Aunty Alice overheard some women talking about a 12 pound 4 ounce baby having been born to which she contributed – 'yes, that's my nephew' before sailing out on a wave of smugness born of knowing something that the gossips didn't).

Apparently being born with a 'veil' over one's face means immunity from drowning and a lucky life to come – perhaps looking back over the big picture that has proved to be true – but I sometimes feel that some of the individual brush strokes leave a lot to be desired. Perhaps then it is true, but luck, like beauty really is in the eye of the beholder – other less fortunate outside observers might see only the positive in another person's life, choosing to envy the good aspects and ignore the others. What I believe is that objectivity is difficult at times and it is not possible to see yourself as others see you.

So there I was, big enough to fill the wicker clothes basket and apparently in need of oxygen, and presumably wondering what life would hold as I joined Mam (Isabella; or Belle to Dad), Dad (James; or Jimmy to Mam), and my three sisters (Isabel, Barbara and Elizabeth, all of us born roughly 4 years apart as a good Catholic family should be...)to complete our family. We would have had another older sibling but she was stillborn at full term.

Of course these earliest memories are borrowed, they are not mine directly.

It seems to me that certain things pass into fact if they are repeated often enough. But really, constant repetition makes it difficult to decide, looking back, how much of your memories are first hand and how many bear embellishments of other people's memories. In the end I suppose that doesn't really matter. If a recollection is how life was seen by another member of your family then it has validity and is quite a nice present of the past that you can recount in the future to anyone who will listen.

A lot of the memories of the earliest years are drawn from small black and white photos, often with Dad's shadow in them as we squinted into the sun shining over his shoulder. I still have his old box camera to this day.

I'm not sure when exactly, but we moved to a colliery house when I was still a toddler. Mam was upset by the house offered as the street was colloquially known as 'dirty Pont', referring to the reputation of the street and the calibre of the inhabitants. But the economic advantages overcame any misgivings – lower rent and free coal. It was one of the perks of being a miner to qualify for a colliery house.

Dad was a miner, and a good one by all accounts. He spent long hours working in seams no more than eighteen inches high, taking pride in hard work and enjoying the competition between different teams. I suppose he was a stereotypical northerner who worked hard and played hard.

Mam kept the family home, a job equally hard but not as valued by society although by my observations it seemed to be a more continuous occupation than any other I can name.

When we first moved in it was a straightforward two up and two down. Literally a kitchen that opened straight off the back door, a front room ('the room' as it was called), and two bedrooms. There was a small thin pantry in the kitchen and a short corridor, with an under stair cupboard, which connected the kitchen to the room. As we got older dad decided to partition the bedroom to accommodate me and my sisters. It was all stud partition, hardboard and then finished tastefully in woodchip wallpaper.

The 'street' that was Pont Street was actually at the back of the house (where the front door was) and the front of the house, accessed by the back door, faced the row of outside toilets and coal houses. The 'street' therefore was a space of small pocket sized gardens and an unpaved pathway. The front door was only used for leaving the house feet first.

There was a fireplace in each of the four rooms and I often wondered what that would be like, having a cheerful fire to warm each room, but never found out as the upstairs ones were soon bricked up by Dad to save on fuel and reduce drafts. The one in the kitchen though was a huge black range, complete with back boiler to supply the hot water, that included compartments for baking and a ledge for heating the flat iron. It dominated the small room. Above the fire was a hook on which you could attach a pan to boil water.

Outside on the wall, as with every house in the street, hung a tin bath.

In the corner of the kitchen was an electric cooker and space for the wash tub and mangle. Apart from that there was limited access to electricity. Later there was a socket for the TV but usually Mam made do with an adapter that allowed appliances to be plugged in alongside a lightbulb.

The steep stairs ran up from the front door (yes, the one at the back of the house) to the landing where the doors to the two bedrooms were. The stairs were against the outside wall as our house was a gable end in one of the many rows of colliery houses and was always cold and damp no matter what Dad applied to try and combat it.

Although the street were long terraces running north to south they were also split at right angles by numbered avenues. Ours ran up to a few shops at one end and then into 'the flower park' which was a haven of beauty in a sea of grey.

We children started off in one large bed – girls at the top and me at the bottom. The toilet was either the 'potty' (some people call them a 'guzzunder' because it goes under the bed) or a very cold trip outside. Of course using the 'guzzunder' or 'po' as it was usually called merely postponed the trip outside to empty it next morning.

Bath night coincided with nit night. A bath in front of the fire for the girls – the wooden clothes horse deployed as a modesty screen, and me in the kitchen sink. Afterward the nit comb painfully untangled the hair as it dried in front of the fire. Our hair was always combed over a sheet of newspaper to make it easier to see any lice or eggs that the comb located.

Of course Dad had more baths as, being a miner, no matter how well he showered at the pit he still needed a good scrub to clean the ingrained dust from his neck.

The street was indeed dirty. But so was almost all of the town – the smoke and soot from the constant fires that provided the only source of heating deposited a blanket of smog, smoke or soot that covered everything in a universal dreariness. This was made worse by deliberate chimney fires caused by an ability to afford a sweep and, when combined with fog and the right atmospheric circumstances produced a pea soup of swirling mists that London would have been proud of.

When we did get a TV the means of changing channel was a large switch on the windowsill where the aerial cable came through the hole drilled into the wooden frame. I was the remote control – not too onerous; especially as there were only three channels – BBC1, BBC 2 (which didn't start until 1964) and ITV, but it did take you away from the warmth of the fire.

The moon landing happened just after 8 p.m.20th July 1969 and Neil Armstrong stepped out in the early hours of Monday 21st. I remember staying up with Dad to watch the landing but I probably didn't stay up quite as long as I remember.

Around that time one of our neighbours had the first colour TV in the street and we boys would crowd around the window to see

High Chapperal, trying and failing to lip read what was happening on the screen. It was a while before we upgraded to colour – our TV was a rented one, and I remember happily watching snooker on TV in black and white up until then. When Ted Lowe announced, 'and for those of you who are watching in black and white, the pink is next to the green', it made perfect sense at the time.

From the time Dad taught me how to play snooker at the 'institute' around the age of 11 I was hooked. It was easy to get into the correct position low over the table as if you didn't your head was in the haze of smoke that constantly hung over every table fed by the cigarettes and pipes of the spectators.

I continued to be hooked on snooker and billiards until pool tables arrived. The first ones were those that had the white larger than the rest of the balls and this provided difficulties when trying to apply back spin. But after a snooker table it was really easy to play. When the next generation arrived, with the white being slightly smaller than the rest of the balls it gave much more scope for clever shots, and the game just got easier still.

I once won the annual knock out competition at one of the working men's clubs, when I was about 21 years old. I hadn't expected to make the final and it was on the same day as the semis. I had expected to be knocked out in my semi match and still have time to get to work. But I ended up winning and going on to the final. This gave me a dilemma until I figured out that the prize for first place was more than I would lose if I was docked a days pay. So I called in sick, played, won, and got paid as well...

Christmas was always nice – I really liked going to midnight mass as I got older – but new year was always more sociable. The drop leaf table in the room was extended and used for the buffet and drinks. We would go first foot up the street before ending up with family and neighbours back at ours where Dad would dance and sing to Frank Ifield (Dad thought that Frank Ifield was great, and he thought the opposite of Fred Astaire) before invariably knocking the Christmas tree over with a flailing arm or leg. As I got older I liked to be alone in front of the fire and enjoy the silence as everyone went next door then I would catch them up. I never got the obsession with mistletoe.

I managed to finally get an Action man for Christmas one year after putting up with the cheaper versions that did not bend. Dad couldn't cope with me wanting to play with a doll.

Christmas was all about tradition – one walnut, one hazelnut, one brazil nut, and a satsuma in each of our socks that were hung from the mantelpiece, despite never eating a single item. A box of Black Magic for Mam, a tin of Tom Thumb cigars and a half bottle of White Horse whisky for Dad.

Sunday lunch was also a tradition. Always chicken as the centrepiece. Always ready and on the table for half past 12 even though Dad never got back from the club before 1.30. I would usually go for 11 o'clock mass and pop in to see my aunty on the way home to read the Broons and Oor Wullie in her copy of the Sunday Post. There was always a loaf of bread proving on the mantel and often a tray of bonfire toffee.

If you look into the history of Ashington you will see that, at the behest of the mine owner, it was for a period tee-total. But that changed over time. A large section of the population were of Irish and Italian descent and consequently catholic. I remember clearly the religious procession of worshippers leaving the church and then the equally reverent procession of men off to the Catholic club or one of the many working men's clubs.

Prior to the miner's picnic the Ashington bands would parade down the avenue before bussing over to Bedlington to join the other colliery bands. We always had a good preview as well as attending the main event, and I was always impressed by the ornate banners, as proudly carried as regimental colours.

Dad had two solidly square leather armchairs which took pride of place in the house – one in the kitchen and the other in the room. The arms were flat and wide enough to eat off and, even if they seemed the most uncomfortable things to sit in, everyone wanted to whenever Dad wasn't there. The one in the room was positioned so that Dad could rest his heels on the mantel piece, a position that seemed to add to the discomfort of the chair but one he seemed to find acceptable.

When it came time to have the house modernised (in the mid to late sixties) one of the tasks in preparation was to scrape the accumulated layers of lino off the kitchen floor. This was a task I enthusiastically launched into along with an old blunt knife to prise it from the floor. In this I was helped by my new friend R who lived in the next gable end house across the avenue.

Out came the marvellous old fireplace in the kitchen and in went a characterless modern smaller tiled affair. Luckily the substantial fireplace in the room was retained.

Half of the pantry disappeared to provide an indoor coal store which was filled via a shuttered outside hole in the wall. Mam and Dad lost some of their bedroom to accommodate the indoor bathroom (a bath *and* toilet!) and airing cupboard. We even got additional electric wall sockets in every room and hot water taps!

But all the time we lived there we never reached the heights of fitted carpets, central heating or double glazing. Ice on the inside of windows in winter was not uncommon and getting dressed in the morning often involved having to warm your clothes up in bed before getting out and putting them on.

And as for a phone – we didn't have mobile phones. We didn't even have a land line. Why bother when there was a phone box across the road. And beside who would we phone as we didn't know anyone who had one. If we wanted to call someone you had to have organised it in advance and use the phone box.

Mam continued to use a small boiler with a mangle on top for the washing. If the weather permitted, the clothes could hang out to dry (cleaning the washing line first to get rid of soot) and if not it was done on the clothes horse in front of the fire. Years later we upgraded to a twin tub washer with a spinner so we didn't need to use the mangle any more.

And then we got to a real state of luxury – getting rid of the large concrete block from the pantry that served to keep things cool and replacing that with a second hand fridge.

As cars gradually invaded our world until they became almost the norm it was time for the rows of outdoor toilets and coal houses to be demolished. They were replaced with a raised hard standing strip of tarmac that eventually became the equivalent of off road parking.

More importantly we discovered a new world – the back of the row of shops! We had often played on the flat roofs of the toilets but rarely had seen any of the people who lived on the other side. How small our world was in those days.

But all that changed when the buildings came down and our embryonic gang of boys ended up with a new member – the son of the butcher. Now the 'gang' had five members along with me, R, A, C and S.

One of the things that I do remember is the regular deliveries of the Rington's tea man, and the almost constant cups of tea consumed in the house. Loose leaves might be authentic but they have drawbacks. No matter how carefully the strainer is used there are always a few leaves floating on the surface of the brew. This was no problem to Dad though – he would scoop them out with his spoon and then flick them into the fire – often missing to Mam's annoyance and the regular cry of, 'Jimmy, I wish you wouldn't do that!'

It is unclear where I got my love of reading from. Books weren't generally in evidence in our house but once the bug bit me I couldn't stop. I remember clearly an early interest in comics and loved the regular trips to the barber with Dad (steadfastly ignoring his lack of hair; he was almost bald from about 21 years of age) where I could read and re-read Superman comics (The local barber was also a Black belt in Judo. He wasn't great at cutting hair but no one complained). But I also clearly remember the first book I read through in one afternoon. It was an abridged version of A Princess of Mars by Edgar Rice Burroughs. After that I worked my way through his entire work. He is a terrible writer but a great storyteller.

Ever since then I've been a serial reader as I discovered other authors and then searched out everything they wrote.

Mealtimes were regular and meals were fairly standard. Toast on the fire for breakfast, egg, chips and beans was for tea and supper was more toast. Treat's were fry ups, fish and chips, stottie cakes, and toasted teacakes. Each teacake was always cut into three slices to make them go further. I was married before I knew that you were allowed a whole one on its own.

Whenever the coal was delivered was always a fun day. To begin with there didn't seem to be a schedule. It arrived when it arrived. If you were in then you could have it emptied straight into the coal house via the hole in the wall. If not it was dumped in the street and you had to shovel it in yourself later. First it would be delivered by horse drawn carts in bags (the coal was in the bags not the horse drawn carts). The horses providing additional treats for keen gardeners. Pooh for the gardens and allotments was a treasured side product of the horses used to deliver coal and also to collect rubbish when the rag and bone man came around. He made profit from your scrap and in return you got a balloon

Later it came in a lorry with a conveyor belt. Most of it hit the target but any that fell off the belt was fair game for widows who no longer received sufficient coal if you didn't scoop it up quickly enough.

To keep it in the coal house and avoid it falling into the kitchen when you opened the door Dad had a system of planks that had to be fitted as the level rose. Another good reason not to invest in fitted carpets.

If you were really unlucky they delivered the coal through the hole in the wall when you were out. Not being there to fit the retaining planks meant that when you opened the internal door a stream of coal fell into the kitchen.

We rarely used logs or sticks – Mam used twists of paper and a 'bleezer' (a metal screen placed in front of the fire to help it take hold) to start a fire, covering any gaps with newspaper to encourage the fire to draw and leap into life. The kitchen fire however rarely went out so didn't have to be lit often from scratch. It would usually just be 'banked up' at night and covered with a layer of ash to restrict the combustion. It would last to the next morning when new coal and application of the bleezer would rapidly bring it roaring back to life.

Unlike modern times when we are so conscious of the impact of our use of plastic and every house on the planet has at least three plastic bins we only every had one. It was mainly full of ash (it was a metal bin of course). It was sufficient as we didn't have as much packaging then and most of it went on the fire.

Infant School.

My first day at St. Aidan's Catholic Infant School (which was later used as a school for unruly boys...) was rather daunting.

It began with an unexpectedly unruly crowd of other children and their mothers gathering in the play ground and was followed by an unceremonious breaking of the apron strings as we were handed over to the old woman dressed all in black who was to be our teacher.

The unremitting concentration on teaching the catechism to be learned by rote should have given me a clue as to what lay ahead.

The school consisted of a number of timber built buildings and stood between the junior school, and the cemetery. The church and the rather grand house that the priests lived in was on the far side of the junior school.

It was inevitable that such proximity to a graveyard bred spooky stories – many of which concerned the large stone tomb that stood in the centre of the churchyard – it was big enough to house a horse and the tale went that it indeed contained not just a deceased person but the remains of his horse. Years later we would dare each other to place an ear to the cold stone where it was reported that one could hear the hooves clattering inside the tomb. Hearing this or not we made many a quick exit in direct contrast to any earlier display of bravado.

There is photographic evidence of us all in angelic poses when we reached the occasion of our first Holy Communion. Looking at the photo now it is difficult to believe that some of the faces staring back over hands pressed together in an attitude of prayer, would presumably belong to heroes or villains as life dealt its cards without reference to mere human wishes or desires.

From an early age one of the accepted treats reserved for me was taking back empty bottles to the shop and being allowed to keep the money. One day though it wasn't really worth it as the consequences outweighed any gain. In my excitement I had grasped the bottles and ran toward the door, ignoring my toy fort and soldiers in my path. Inevitably the resulting tumble among broken shards of glass led to a deep laceration.

I had cut my index finger to the bone and still bear the scar. Dad being Dad simply applied plaster after plaster until it stopped bleeding.

Thunder and lightning are natural phenomena but mam and Aunty Alice were both terrified of it. Their less than scientific remedy to it was to open the front and back windows (so it could go straight through), switch off everything electric apart from the radio – and sit in the cupboard under the stairs.

This seemed as likely to work as some of mam's other life lessons – Brown paper and butter for a black eye, trusting Whittaker's almanac, and quoting 'when one door closes another one opens'.

Toward the end of my time at infant school I was admitted to the Hospital at Blyth to have my tonsils removed. It was winter and there was a lot of snow so it was difficult for Mam and Dad to visit as the buses weren't that regular and the weather made things worse. I do remember one visit where one of the other boys received a toy car as a present from his parents. Dad was feeling kind and offered to go and buy one for me but after a fruitless search he returned empty handed and covered in snow.

My other abiding memory of that stay in hospital was of a nurse who gave me a drink, stating that it was milk. The majority was but it also contained antibiotics, whose taste could not be disguised that easily. I never trusted doctors or nurses after that.

My time at infant school passed quickly and soon I was in the final year, watching from a vantage point of experience the delivery of new infants at the start of the school year. This final year brought me to the dizzying height of water monitor for our table at lunchtime!

Junior school

St Aidan's Junior school was directly opposite entrance to the infants school. In distance only the width of a road, but in imagination the gap was enormous. It had a high wall and a set of metal gates. The other entrance around the back was a small gate leading directly to the house where the Priest's lived, beyond which was the church.

I liked Saturdays. Mostly because, if Dad's luck was in I would get enough pocket money to buy a new soldier or cowboy from the toy shop around the corner. If I was really lucky I got enough to buy one on horseback. An ironic link given that the source of my good fortune rested on the winnings from horse racing. Dad liked a drink and Saturday afternoon betting on the horses. If he won I got more pocket money.

Dad would study the form, sort out his bets, usually some form of accumulator, and then walk around to the betting shop to place his wager. He also liked football and was a regular contributor to the pools.

As children we hadn't yet acquired a consistent or grown up perspective on right and wrong. The gardens behind the houses were often filled with the accumulated detritus of man, discarded items out of sight and therefore out of mind. Rusty bath tubs, no longer needed due to the indoor plumbing, rotted quietly away and provided excellent breeding grounds for earwigs, known to us as 'forky tails'. These poor creatures did not attract the same sacred status as other living creatures in our developing minds and through some perverted logic on our part were legitimate targets for our harassment. Our 'gang' would spend many happy hours hunting them down and then attacking from different directions with washing up liquid bottles filled with water which could fire concentrated jets of water over reasonable distances with various degrees of accuracy.

But it was a lot safer to play out then as there were hardly any cars. Until the toilets were demolished to make parking spaces as much as to provide indoor facilities.

Overall I was an average student but did make Prefect in my last year. The responsibilities attached to this position of authority seemed to consist of keeping a watch on the caretakers ladders at play time.

I remember working on the school Radio, being sent to the Headmaster with a poem I had written that the teacher thought he should see, dark afternoons with rain rattling on the panes, mental arithmetic tests (which I still can't do) and the religious aspects of that period of my education.

On Monday morning the priest would visit each classroom to check that we had all been to church the day before. We would also be marched around to church each Friday and also to confession on Wednesday.

I spent some time as an altar boy which was profitable (not having to put in the plate), them I joined the choir (as I had read about a free choir trip to the zoo).

Sometimes I would have the company of my sister Liz on Sunday to go to church. If we were a little late Mam would find some money for the bus. We would then run to the next stop or the one after that if we were lucky and keep the change.

Guy Fawkes and penny for the guy were good ways to supplement income, more so if you collared the drunks as they left the pub.

Christmas carolling was another way we tried to defraud the public of their money.

Eventually I followed in Liz's footsteps by passing my 11 plus and going up to the Grammar school. Risking the ire of the priests of course who threatened excommunication to those who attended the non Catholic school.

I suppose I was around 5 when Isabel left to get married and perhaps 11 or 12 when Barb did. Liz joined up when I was 12 also so after that I was on my own with Mam and Dad.

Grammar school

Grammar school was ok. I was top of my year in maths at the end of the first year, second in maths at the end of the second year. It all went downhill after that.

I hated team sports, hated dancing at the school dance, (but perversely pestered for a cravat to go to 'the hop'). I really hated having free school meals.

The Grammar school went Comprehensive from year three and I then discovered that I hated fighting. Being able to do something doesn't mean that you should or have to.

As the final year approached we were treated to a short meeting with the school career adviser. Mine was very short. According to him my options were the pit or the forces. Pit was out as my Dad had decided that so that left the forces. The question then was which one.

My sister had joined the Navy. Of the rest of our 'gang' one wanted to be a Marine, one wanted to join the RAF but R and I wanted the Navy. R's oldest brother had joined the Merchant Navy and his next oldest was in the Navy.

We went to the selection day together (bend over and cough...) and the entrance exams seemed a bit too easy to me, with most of them being multi choice.

I was successful.

R failed the basic exam three times so couldn't join up. Instead he became a soldier.

So I left school and waited to join while watching a documentary series about HMS Ark Royal and listening to Rod Stewart sing, 'We are sailing'.

Better that than 'In the Navy' by the Village People.

By now Dad was very ill and I stood in for him at Liz's wedding.

Royal Navy

I travelled to Plymouth by train. The longest distance I had ever been, and certainly one of the first on my own.

Six weeks later we had our 'Passing in Parade' and a year later we had our 'Passing out Parade'.

In between I spent weekends 'ashore' lodging at Aggie Weston's and of course visited Diamond Lil's on Union Street.

The next three years were spent at Rosyth (just over the Forth Road Bridge and turn left) where I spent weekends in Dunfermline eating chips, burger and beans, visiting the cinema to enjoy such classics as Saturday Night Fever and visiting discotheques that served portions of haggis, tatties and neeps at midnight as part of the entrance price.

A key lesson that I learned was that it it moves you salute it and if it doesn't you paint it white. That and 'never volunteer'.

Unemployment

My one brief period of worklessness was not something that I planned to repeat. For a start you don't get a lot of money; enough for one pint, one bag of crisps and one game of pool a night if you are lucky.

When Mam suggested I could now put my name down for a council house I knew it was time to move on.

So I applied to be a psychiatric nurse.

Printed in Great Britain
by Amazon